Concealed
in
Sight

The Bloodline Israelites

D1563454

Concealed In Sight

Hugh Saddler

"Sh'ma Yisrael YHWH Eloheinu YHWH Echad"[1]

ISBN: 9798595987851

---

[1] Shema

CONTENTS

INTRODUCTION

There are many discussions today regarding the biblical Israelites, and who they were as a people. These conversations involve migration patterns, spiritual practices, and changes, did those practices change with time, and if so, who authorized the change? The most contested topic argued today regarding the Israelites is their race and complexion. What was the race of the Israelites, and more importantly, how did they describe themselves? Within these discussions, once the racial component appears to be resolved, the additional question inevitably becomes who, and where, are these people today. The debate of the race of the Israelites is very much a political one, and is clearly not rooted in Torah, or Talmud.

Both the Torah and Talmud, and for the sake of this conversation, the whole Tanakh, and pretty much all the spiritual texts, along with historical accounts, are quite clear regarding this issue. These texts also provide evidence as to who the Israelites are today.

Were the Biblical Israelites a Caucasian, pale complexioned people, or were they a deeply melanated Afro-Asiatic black people? The Torah is believed to be the foundation of Abrahamic faith, and outlines the history of the Israelites as a people, it must be examined correctly to properly identify this nation. In addition to Torah, the Talmudic traditions must be closely examined to see if there is any evidence that identifies them. Lastly, dates, and timelines need to be established. One must consider how this nation of people were identified by their contemporary nations, and any information or writings must be considered tertiary evidence to assist in establishing their true identity.

Several attempts have been made to address this topic of their identity. For example, lectures have been given, and there have been several books written about it. It is an honor, and I feel it is my duty to present evidence that will put this conversation to rest! This book will produce evidence that the

1

previous champions of this discussion may have overlooked, and provide information that may not have been previously made available to them. It will also provide evidence from the Torah, Talmudic traditions, several passages from the Prophets, and the Ketuvim as evidence; as well as the contemporary nations artifacts, paintings, and writings that would beyond a shadow of doubt, end this discussion for good.

"ALL Praise is due to thee Hashem and YOU alone! It is YOU, and YOU alone who is master of the day of judgment, KING of all kings, Lord of all the worlds, and Lord of all creation. You neither beget, nor are you begotten, nor do you have any partners. You share your glory and praise with no one, for there is nothing like you!"[2]

---

[2] Personal Prayer 2

CONTEXT

According to the book of Genesis Noah had three sons. Ham, Shem, and Japheth[3]. It is important to examine this chapter with Talmudic traditions in the forefront of your mind while reading. The description of the sons of Noah can be found in the Talmud. There is a rabbinical tradition that describes the complexion of the sons of Noah. The tradition states that Noah blessed Shem whose physical appearance was black, but comely. Noah blessed Ham, and his complexion was described as being black as a raven. Lastly, Noah blessed Japheth but described him as being morally unworthy, and shamed with entirely white complexion.[4]

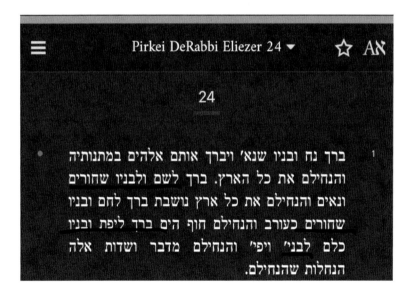

≡   Pirkei DeRabbi Eliezer 24 ▾   ☆ אA

24

ברך נח ובניו שנא' ויברך אותם אלהים במתנותיה   1
והנחילם את כל הארץ. ברך לשם ולבניו שחורים
נאים והנחילם את כל ארץ נושבת ברך לחם ובניו
שחורים כעורב והנחילם חוף הים ברד ליפת ובניו
כלם לבני' ויפי' והנחילם מדבר ושדות אלה
הנחלות שהנחילם.

---

[3] Genesis 6:10

[4] Talmud: Pirkei DeRabbi Eliezer 24:1

When describing Japheth, the Hebrew word for shamed is used[5].

In the year circa 3890 BC Noah was born. Noah lived approximately 500 years prior to the great flooding of the earth. It is important to quickly examine how the inhabitants of the earth were described, and the sentiments regarding those descriptions according to several spiritual texts. According to rabbinical tradition, if someone was born with a white complexion, it was believed to have been born by angelic beings, who were also called sons of god.

It is rabbinical tradition that when someone was born with white complexion, it was seen as either abnormal, unnatural, or unearthly. This perspective manifests itself in nature according to rabbinical tradition.

> The Holy One, blessed be He, gave a good reward to the ravens in this world. What reward did He give them? When they bear their young and see that they are white they fly from them, thinking that they are the offspring of a serpent, and the Holy One, blessed be He, gives them their sustenance without lack, as it is said, "Who provideth for the raven his food, when his young ones cry unto God, and wander for lack of meat" (Job 38:41). Moreover, that rain should be given upon the earth (for their sakes), and the Holy One, blessed be He, answers them, as it is said, "He giveth to the beast his food, and to the young ravens which cry" (Ps. 147:9). [6]

---

[5] Etymological Dictionary of Biblical Hebrew

[6] Rabbinical Tradition: Pirkei DeRabbi Eliezer 21:10

It is also rabbinical tradition that Cain was a product of this type of relationship, and he was not the seed of Adam. It is said that Cain is the seed of a fallen angel, and had a twin sister, who was also not Adam's seed.

≡   Pirkei DeRabbi Eliezer 22 ∨   ☆ Aℵ

THE FALL OF THE ANGELS

"AND Adam lived an hundred and thirty years, and he begat in his own likeness after his image" (**Gen. 5:3**). Hence thou mayest learn that Cain was not of Adam's seed, nor after his likeness, nor after his image. (Adam did not beget in his own image) until Seth was born, who was after his father Adam's likeness and image, as it is said, "And he begat in his own likeness, after his image" (*ibid.*).

[7]

Based on rabbinical tradition, one could conclude that prior to the flood of the earth, white complexion was associated with ungodliness, violence, and wickedness. Something or a people unholy, for it is written:

---

[7] Rabbinical Tradition, Pirkei DeRabbi Eliezer 22:1

2 Rabbi Simeon said: From Seth arose and were descended all the generations of the righteous. From Cain arose and were descended all the generations of the wicked, who rebel and sin, who rebelled against their Rock, and they said: We do not need the drops of Thy rain, neither to walk in Thy ways, as it is said, "Yet they said unto God, Depart from us" (Job 21:14).

3 Rabbi Meir said: || The generations of Cain went about stark naked, men and women, just like the beasts, and they defiled themselves with all kinds of immorality, a man with his mother or his daughter, or the wife of his brother, or the wife of his neighbour, in public and in the streets, with evil inclination which is in the thought of their heart, as it is said, "And the Lord saw that the wickedness of man was great in the earth" (Gen. 6:5).

8

In addition to the Talmudic traditions regarding the whiteness of Cain, Author Damon stated in his book titled, 'The Book Of Lamech Of Cain', that Cain was cursed with White complexion, and this "curse" would be upon his children forever[9]. The negative sentiment surrounding white complexion can also be found in the story of Noah himself. Lamech, the Father of Noah, believed Noah to be the progeny of fallen angels. So much so, that he asked his father Methuselah to contact Enoch to help explain his white complexion to him. Noah is described as having a body that was white as snow, and hair

8 Rabbinical Tradition, Pirkei DeRabbi Eliezer 22:2

9 The Book Of Lamech of Cain, Ch: 1 verse 4

that was white as wool[10]. What is interesting to note here is that Lameck pleaded with Methuselah stating that this child is unlike man, making a clear distinction between Both black and white complexions.

To be clear and to establish contexts before moving forward to the sons of Noah, we have the books of Enoch, the book of the Lameck of Cain, and we have rabbinical traditions that establish the white complexion being something other than the natural black complexion of Adam and his sons.

Again I have 4 points to establish before further analyzing the book of Genesis:

1. I have evidence of sentiment regarding white complexion in a book that the author says was commissioned by the Vatican in 2019. This book highlights and gives a very particular description of Cain being described as cursed to be white with leprosy; A complexion that we will find to be synonymous with a curse throughout the Torah.

2. I have Talmudic traditions that establish that the Israelites were a black, but comely. It was Japheth who was the white albino of the 3 sons of Noah.

3. The Book of Enoch additionally illustrates the sentiment regarding white complexion. Lamech, the father of Noah, believed that he was not his son, but rather the son of a fallen angel, because he was white complexioned.

4. The Talmudic traditions support the story of white complexion being something other than that of the Israelites.

---

[10] The Book of Enoch, Ch: 106

In the year circa 5400 BC, Cain resided in the city of Nod[11], and this city consisted of all of his progeny, and children of the fallen angels. According to the sources mentioned above, these were white complexioned people. In the years circa 3890 BC, Noah's complexion had been identified as being white. His father, Methuselah, was a black man from the lineage of Seth, who was the son of Adam. So with Noah being an albino, we see the phenomenon of him having two black sons and one Albino Japheth.

---

[11] KJV Bible Genesis 4:16

Lastly, to clear up any confusion about leprosy. Some attempt to argue that it is a scaly skin affliction, while Rabbinical tradition identifies it as plainly as white appearance[12].

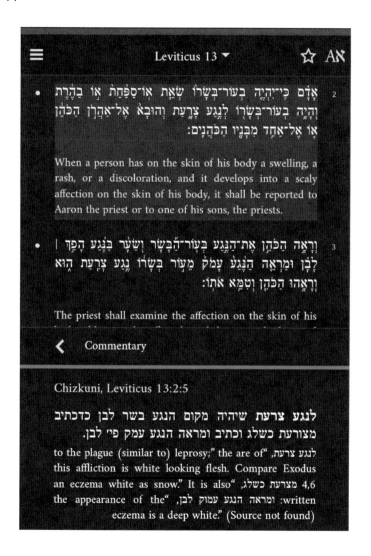

אָדָם כִּי־יִהְיֶה בְעוֹר־בְּשָׂרוֹ שְׂאֵת אוֹ־סַפַּחַת אוֹ בַהֶרֶת 2
וְהָיָה בְעוֹר־בְּשָׂרוֹ לְנֶגַע צָרָעַת וְהוּבָא אֶל־אַהֲרֹן הַכֹּהֵן
אוֹ אֶל־אַחַד מִבָּנָיו הַכֹּהֲנִים:

When a person has on the skin of his body a swelling, a rash, or a discoloration, and it develops into a scaly affection on the skin of his body, it shall be reported to Aaron the priest or to one of his sons, the priests.

וְרָאָה הַכֹּהֵן אֶת־הַנֶּגַע בְּעוֹר־הַבָּשָׂר וְשֵׂעָר בַּנֶּגַע הָפַךְ | 3
לָבָן וּמַרְאֵה הַנֶּגַע עָמֹק מֵעוֹר בְּשָׂרוֹ נֶגַע צָרַעַת הוּא
וְרָאָהוּ הַכֹּהֵן וְטִמֵּא אֹתוֹ:

The priest shall examine the affection on the skin of his

❮ Commentary

Chizkuni, Leviticus 13:2:5

לנגע צרעת שיהיה מקום הנגע בשר לבן כדכתיב
מצורעת כשלג וכתיב ומראה הנגע עמק פי' לבן.

to the plague (similar to) leprosy;" the are of" ,לנגע צרעת
this affliction is white looking flesh. Compare Exodus
an eczema white as snow." It is also" ,מצרעת כשלג 4,6
the appearance of the" ,ומראה הנגע עמוק לבן written: ומראה הנגע עמוק לבן
eczema is a deep white." (Source not found)

---

[12] Rabbinical Commentary on Torah: Chizkuni, Leviticus 13:2

GENESIS

In the year circa 3300 BC, after the flood, Noah blessed his sons and gave them their inhabitable portions of the land. It is then that his sons began to multiply on the earth. Talmudic tradition state that they multiplied in pairs of sixes[13].

> RABBI ELIEZER said: They begat their sons and increased and multiplied like a great reptile, six at each birth, and they were all one people, and one heart, and one language, as it is said, "And the whole earth was of one language and of one speech" (Gen. 11:1). They despised the pleasant land, as it is said, "And it came to pass, as they journeyed in the east" (Gen. 11:2). They went to the land of Shinar, and found there a large stone, very extensive, and the whole plain, and they dwelt there, as it is said, "And they found a plain in the land of Shinar, and they dwelt there" (ibid.).

In the years of post flood, circa 3270 BC, it is really important for the reader to understand that Japheth's wife Arbasisah, was a direct descendant of Cain. In the book of Genesis, Noah's son, Japheth, and his children are mentioned. Genesis 10:1-5 reads:

Now these are the generations of the sons of Noah, Shem, Ham, and Japheth: and unto them were sons born after the flood. 2 The sons of Japheth; Gomer, and Magog, and Madai, and Javan, and Tubal, and Meshech, and Tiras. 3 And the sons of Gomer; Ashkenaz, and Riphath,and

---

13 Talmudic tradition: Pirkiei DeRabbi Eliezer 24:2

Togarmah. 4 And the sons of Javan; Elishah, and Tarshish, Kittim, and Dodanim. 5 By these were the Gentiles divided in their lands; every one after his tongue, after their families, in their nations.[14]

Previously written, Cain is the progeny of a fallen angel, and Eve, and the complexion of such a union was white. Now, Torah identifies Japheth's descendants as being gentiles. Talmudic, Rabbinical tradition, confirms the complexion of Japheth's descendants as being white complexioned people. White complexion being established, and reserved for Japheth. Now, attention is given to the complexion of both Ham, and Shem. Ham's complexion was described as being black as a raven[15], and Shem's complexion was described as being Black and Comely.[16] This is a synonym for beautiful. Shem lived within the borders of Ham.

In the 10th chapter of the book of Genesis, verses 6-30 identifies the progeny of both Ham and Shem, being born circa 3100 BC. It also informs us when the earth was divided[17]. In the book of Genesis, chapter 11:27, records the birth of Abraham. Abraham was born approximately 500 years after the birth of the Sons of Noah. For beyond a shadow of a doubt, there is no Japhetic nation that can claim that they are the seed of Abraham. Abraham is not the father of any Hamitic nation neither. Abraham was from the lineage of Shem, and he lived within the borders of Hamitic people.

The specific Hamitic people with whom Abraham lived, were the Cushite people. They procreated in, and occupied the land of Shinar. The Cushite people were a very black people who populated this area of land, and they were ruled by Nimrod the great.[18] According to both Torah, and Talmudic

---

[14] KJV Bible Genesis 10:1-5

[15] Pirkei DeRabbi Eliezer 24:1

[16] Ibid

[17] KJV Bible Genesis 10:25

[18] KJV Bible Genesis 10:8-11

traditions, this area of land was populated by very black people, who were also ruled approximately 500 years prior to the birth of Abraham, by a very Black Cushite King, named Nimrod.

Abraham, was a black and comely/beautiful descendent of Shem. He migrated from Ur of the Chaldees, which was within the borders of the Kingdom of Babylon. Abraham was accompanied by his black and beautiful wife, Sarah, on their long migration into the land of Canaan. Both Torah, and Talmud, identify Canaan as being the son of Ham, who was as black as a raven[19]. According to Rabbinical tradition, and Torah, the whole areas in which Abraham traveled were controlled, and occupied by black people. Once in the land of Canaan, G-D appeared to Abraham, and told him "...unto thy seed will i give this land..."[20]. While in the land of Canaan on another occasion, G-D appeared unto Abraham, and told him, "I am the Almighty God, walk before me, and be perfect"...and Abram fell on his face to pray"[21].

In Genesis 15:13, G-D told Abraham to know of a surety that your descendants should be enslaved in the land that is not theirs, and they shall serve and afflict them for 400 years. G-D goes on to say in Genesis, verses 15:14, that nation that has afflicted them HE will punish, and the Israelites will come out with great substance.

Torah states that Sarah, Abraham's Black wife, gave him her Egyptian black handmade/servant as a second wife[22]. The servant that Sarah gave Abraham to be his second wife, was Hagar the black Egyptian. Hagar is the mother of Ishmael, the firstborn son of Abraham. Again, the Semitic(of Shem) Abraham was black and beautiful. Hagar, his second wife, was a

---

[19] Pirkei DeRabbi Eliezer 24:1

[20] KJV Bible Genesis 12:7

[21] KJV Bible Genesis 17:1-3

[22] KJV Bible Genesis 16:3

Hamitic Egyptian, who was black as a raven. Ishmael was a mixture of Black and beautiful, and Black as a raven, which would ultimately make him deep black in complexion.

In Genesis chapter 17, in verses 1-9, G-D is having a conversation with Abraham regarding his covenant with him. This covenant clarifies the roles of Abraham, and his seed, and it identifies where the manifestation of this covenant were to take place.

The Torah reads:

And when Abram was ninety years old and nine, the Lord appeared to Abram and said unto him, *I AM THE ALMIGHTY G-D; WALK BEFORE ME, AND BE THOU PERFECT. 2 AND I WILL MAKE MY COVENANT BE-TWEEN ME AND THEE, AND I WILL MULTIPLY THEE EXCEEDINGLY. 3 And Abram fell on his face: and G-D talked with him saying, 4 AS FOR ME, BEHOLD, MY COVENANT IS WITH THEE, AND THOU SHALT BE A FA-THER OF MANY NATIONS. 5 NEITHER SHALL THY NAME ANY MORE BE CALLED ABRAM, BUT THY NAME SHALL BE ABRAHAM; FOR A FATHER OF MANY NATIONS HAVE I MADE THEE. 6 AND I WILL MAKE THEE EXCEEDING FRUITFUL, AND I WILL MAKE NATIONS OF THEE, AND KINGS SHALL COME OUT OF THEE. 7 AND I WILL ESTABLISH MY COVENANT BETWEEN ME AND THEE AND THY SEED AFTER THEE IN THEIR GENERATIONS FOR AN EVERLASTING COVENANT, TO BE A G-D UNTO THEE, AND TO THY SEED AFTER THEE. 8 AND I WILL GIVE UNTO THEE, AND TO THY SEED AFTER THEE, THE LAND WHEREIN THOU ART A STRANGER, ALL THE LAND OF CANAAN, FOR AN EVER-LASTING POSSESSION; AND I WILL BE THEIR G-D.* 9 And G-D said unto Abraham, *THOU SHALT KEEP MY COVENANT THEREFORE, THOU, AND THY SEED AFTER THEE IN THEIR GENERATIONS.*

When G-D told Abraham that he would be a father of many nations, it's important to know that he was talking about Abraham's progeny; the many nations were to come from Abraham's loins. Abraham obviously cannot be the father of any Hamitic, or Japhetic nation, seeing that they existed

500-800 years before Abraham was born. What is also telling about Hashem's decree to Abraham, was that he told him he would be the G-D to Abraham and ALL his progeny, including his BLACK SON ISHMAEL. He never stated that he will be the G-D to the Japhetic nations, nor to the Hamitic nations.

Though we understand that Hashem is the LORD of ALL creation, this verse denotes a closeness, or a special relationship that he has, and will have with Abraham and his progeny. Hashem decreed that the land of Canaan, was for Abraham and ALL his progeny. After Hashem made his covenant with Abraham, the Black Semitic(of Shem) Sarah, Abraham's wife, birthed Abraham's second son, the Black Semitic Isaac.

In the year circa 2060 BC, Abraham resided in the Black Hamitic land of Canaan with both his Black sons, Ishmael, and Issac. They were birthed to him by black women. Abraham taught his traditions, and covenant to both his sons, and his household. Hashem blessed Ishmael, and said that he will have 12 princes, and he will be a great nation in the earth[23]. Abraham's two sons Ishmael, and Isaac would go on to marry and procreate with both black Hamitic, and Semitic women. Isaac married Rebecca, who was a black Semitic woman, and the granddaughter of his uncle Nahor, Abraham's brother[24]. Ishmael married a black Hamitic woman from Egypt, who was given to him by his mother, Hagar[25].

In the year circa 2006 BC, Isaac and Rebeca gave birth to twin sons Jacob and Esau. Both of these sons were Black; One being reddish, and the other darker black. It is important to note that Abraham had at least 8 sons according to Torah, 6 of them coming from his wife Keturah[26]. There is some

---

[23] KJV Bible Genesis 17:20

[24] KJV Bible Genesis 24:15

[25] KJV Bible Genesis 21:21

[26] KJV Bible Genesis 25:1-2

scholarly debate that asks if Keturah, and Hagar, are the same person. One must examine the marital instructions that Abraham gave to his senior servant(Eliezer), for his son Isaac, and the obedience of Abraham to his G-D. Abraham's only prerequisite for marriage for his sons was that they did NOT marry a Canaanite woman.

For those who may not be familiar with the story of Jacob and Esau, here is a brief summation of their story! Jacob and Esau were prophesied to be two different nations, and there would be enmity between the two nations for many reasons. The primary reason being that Jacob stole the firstborn birthright blessing from Esau[27]. The birthright was for the older to be ruler over the younger, and to have exclusive favor from G-D over all the many nations of Abraham. I understand that there are a lot of people who erroneously say, and believe that Esau was born white, and is the white nation today. Esau is not the white man, nor is he the father of any white nation.

According to Torah, Esau married Ishmael's daughter Mahalath[28], who was the daughter by virtue of Ishmael marrying an Egyptian. Her complexion was between black as a raven, and black and beautiful. Esau also married the daughters of the Canaanites[29], and they dwelled in mount Seir. Mount Seir's location is, and was in southern Jordan, bordering on Egypt, and Arabia; lands that were settled and occupied by black people.

In the year circa 1950 BC, Esau married black nations. He married the Ishmaelite's, Hivites, Hittites, and the progeny of these marriages were black people. All of the nations that sprung forth from the sons of Esau were black nations, so again, it is impossible for Esau, or the Edomites to be a white nation, and especially, not white from birth. To clarify and conclude the discussion regarding Esau, I repeat, Esau is not the father of any white nation,

---

[27] KJV Bible Genesis 27:1-46

[28] KJV Bible Genesis 28:9

[29] KJV Bible Genesis 36:2

neither was he a white, reddish man at birth; rather his complexion had a brownish red hue to it.

Between the years circa 1930-1940 BC, Jacob married both Rachel and Leah. They were black Semitic people through Laban the Syrian, who was the son of Bethuel; who is the son of the union of Milcah, and Nahor, Abraham's brother[30]. Laban is the brother of Rebecca, Jacob's mother, who was Isaac's wife. It is important to note that the Torah refers to Laban as a Syrian[31]. This identity given to Laban is very important to understand, for during the years circa 1930 BC, the Syrian people were black, and the Mishna Torah refers to them as such. These black Semitic, Syriac people, are the matriarchs to the black Semitic Israelite nation. Rachel and Leah, also used their handmaid's Zipah, and Bilah to birth children for them.

Jacob			
Leah (Older Sister)	Zilpah (Leah's Servant)	Bilah (Rachels Servant)	Rachel (Younger Sister)
1. Reuben	7. Gad	5. Dan	11. Joseph
2. Simeon	8. Asher	6. Naphtali	12. Benjamin
3. Levi			
4. Judah			
9. Issachar			
10. Zebulun			
Daughter, Dinah			

As we can see on this chart, it is clear that the 8 sons, and one daughter between both Rachel, and Leah were black. The complexion of the two handmaids Zilpah, and Bilah are unclear, though, there is a midrash that states that they were daughters of Laban[32]. This ultimately would make them

---

[30] KJV Bible Genesis 29:1-35

[31] KJV Bible Genesis 31:24

[32] Gen. Rabbati, Vayeze, p.119

black. However, due to the fact that they were impregnated by Jacob, who was black, the progeny of such a union would undoubtedly be black.

There are some people who describes the story of Jacob, and Rachel, as one of the greatest love stories the world has ever heard, and known[33]; It should be remembered as one of the greatest displays of black love, for all the children of Jacob were black. Jacob whose name was later changed to Israel, had 12 sons, and 1 daughter. They were all deeply melanated, black people.

Joseph, the youngest, and favored child of Jacob/Israel, that he sired by Rachel, was placed in a pit by his brethren due to jealousy. Joseph was ultimately sold to the Black Egyptians, and was able to pass as one of them. Joseph lived amongst the black Egyptians, and was able to move up to the prestigious position as viceroy to Pharaoh Senusret II[34].

During the years circa 1880 BC, there was famine all over the earth. Due to this extreme famine in the land of Canaan, the sons of Jacob/Israel were sent into Egypt to buy grain to be brought back to the land Canaan to sustain their tribe. Once in the Land of Egypt, the sons of Jacob/Israel were brought before Joseph, and they did not recognize their brother. He appeared to be a Black Egyptian. Joseph recognized his brethren because they had full beards[35], and due to Joseph being in the house of Pharaoh, he shaved his beard in order to be identified with the Egyptians. The Hamitic Egyptians at this time were a people who couldn't grow full beards. Joseph revealed himself to his brethren. He ordered them to bring his father, Israel, and his whole household down into Egypt. During the years circa 1876 BC, Israel entered into Black Egypt, and was given the territory of Goshen wherein to reside.

---

[33] Inner Space by Rabbi Aryeh Kaplan pg. 66

[34] KJV Bible Genesis 41:33

[35] Targum Jonathan on Genesis 42:8

During the reign of both Pharaoh's Senusret II, and Amenemhet II, Egypt was a very black nation. As stated earlier in this book, Mizraim/Egypt, is the son of Ham. According to Rabbinical tradition, Ham was black as a raven. As Israel continued to grow and prosper in the land of Egypt, Jacob/Israel blessed his sons, and he died in the years circa 1855-1859 BC[36]. When time came to bury Jacob/Israel, Joseph, and all the elders in the house of Pharaoh, all the elders in the land of Egypt, and all the elders in the house Israel, they loaded up chariots and caravans to go bury Israel in the land of Canaan. Torah describes the scene as being a massive caravan of people, and the Canaanites thought it was an Egyptian funeral[37]. The fact that the Canaanites could not make a distinction between the Israelites, and the Egyptians, is all the evidence one needs as proof that both these nations were deeply melanated black people.

When you examine the book of Genesis, with talmudic descriptions of the children of Noah in mind, you will see that Japheth was a white/albino, and gentile nation. His portion of land was the colder climates of modern day European nations. It is very clear that Ham was a nation that was as black as a raven, and their portion of land was all of Africa, with territories that stretched to Iraq/Babylon. Lastly, you will see that Shem was a black and comely nation, whose portion of land was to include all the land of Canaan, unto the west side of Jordan.

---

[36] Steve Rudd Bible Chronology Chart

[37] KJV Bible Genesis 50:11

EXODUS

In the book of Exodus, the Israelite history resumes during the years circa 1525-1510. During these years, history records that there were several black, Hamitic pharaoh's that reigned, and ruled Egypt[38]. During these years we have the birth of Moses, and him being brought into the house of Pharaoh. Here is evidence of black, Hamitic royalty, embracing a black, Semitic child as their own.

I must repeat, Torah, and Rabbinical tradition, establishes both the Hamitic, and Semitic people as being black. Moses was embraced as a child of Egyptian royalty. Either the Egyptians, and the Israelites were a white complexioned people; A complexion that is identified as Japhetic, and that of falling angels, or they both were black. It is clear that they were not opposites at this point in history.

When Moses was a fugitive, he assisted some young women with watering a herd of sheep. Once their father, a Midianite priest, asked them why they were back so soon from watering the flock, they told him that an Egyptian helped them[39]. Moses married Zipporah, who was the very daughter of that black Semitic, Midianite priest, named Jethro. Moses and Zipporah had a son named Gershom, who no doubt was a black, Semitic child.

In the years circa 1458-1440 BC, According to Torah, G-D had a conversation with Moses. He instructed him on how to interact with Pharaoh Amenhotep II[40]. He informed him of what miracles to perform in order to convince him to free the Israelites. Of the two miracles that were instructed

---

[38] The Prophecy Society of Atlanta, Timeline-Abraham to Solomon

[39] KJV Bible Exodus 2:18-19

[40] Steve Rudd Exodus Timeline Chart

to Moses, the 2nd miracle, when his black hand turned white, was the most profound.

Exodus 4: 6-8 reads:

6 And the Lord said furthermore unto him, *PUT NOW THINE HAND INTO THY BOSOM.* And he put his hand into his bosom: and when he took it out, behold, his hand was white as snow. 7 And he said, PUT THINE HAND INTO THY BOSOM AGAIN. And he put his hand into his bosom again; and plucked it out of his bosom, and behold, it was turned again, as his other flesh. 8 *AND IT SHALL COME TO PASS, IF THEY WILL NOT HEARKEN TO THE VOICE OF THE FIRST SIGN, THAT THEY WILL BE-LIEVE THE VOICE OF THE LATTER SIGN.*

In this verse in the Torah, this is a story within a story. In this story, G-D is certain that if Pharaoh wouldn't believe the first miracle, he most certainly would believe the second one. This illustrates a level of sure shock, or fear the Pharaohs would indeed display at a black man having the ability to change complexions before their eyes. This passage also illustrates that white complexion was not Moses's natural complexion, for his hand "re-turned" as his other flesh; black.

After these miracles were performed, and exiting Egypt, Torah states that there were a mixed multitude that left with Israel[41]. Established earlier, the complexion of all the nations/people that were in this region were black Hamitic, and Semitic people. White, caucasian complexion, during this time was still seen as something uncommon, or unnatural.

The children of Israel, and the mixed multitudes of other black Hamitic, and Semitic people, lived amongst, and procreated with one another during the years in the wilderness. This was before crossing over Jordan into Israel. It is a matter of fact that the progeny of these nations were deeply black

---

[41] KJV Bible Exodus 12:38

melanated people, for Israelites were mistaken for Egyptians, and vice ver-sa. During the years circa 1440-1410 BC, the complexions of all the peoples within their various nations in the North-East African region, as well as all the nations in the Arabian peninsula, were very black. The white complexioned Japhetic nations had yet to enlarge themselves amongst the black Semitic, and Hamitic peoples.

LEVITICUS

Following the Exodus from Egypt, and while traveling in the wilderness of Sinai, G-D gave Moses laws concerning his people. In the book of Leviticus G-D is very clear as to what his order was for his people. The Israelites, and the mixed multitude of people amongst them, were still, and yet remained a black nation while receiving the law. The oral Torah, also known as the Mishna, existed before Moses, and is a necessary book to assist in understanding the book of Leviticus. Of the 5 books of the Torah, Leviticus is arguably the most clear regarding white complexion. The sentiments regarding white complexion are revealed within this book of the law, with razor sharp specificity.

Hashem warns the Israelites not to procreate with other nations, in order to prevent them from losing their customs and traditions, and from following the other nations' practice of worshiping other gods.[42] In the 13th chapter of Leviticus, Hashem begins to address the skin affliction, called leprosy. When the natural black complexion of the Israelites appeared to turn white in any form, they were deemed unclean[43]. There was a 21 day maximum process in which to examine if a white spot on any Israelite would have turned dark, or had a dark undertone to it. If the complexion did not turn dark after the 21 days, you were considered a leper, and Israel was given an order from Hashem to remove those people from the tents, and away from the congregation.

Both chapters, 13, and 14 of the book of Leviticus addresses the concerns, and fears of having white skin. It is clear in these chapters that white complexion was something that was abnormal, and something that was foreign to the black complexion of the Israelites. These chapters say

---

[42] KJV Bible Exodus 34:14-16

[43] KJV Bible Leviticus 13:1-3

that you were unclean if you had whiteness in your flesh. This is another clear indicator that during the years of Moses, the complexion of the people in the whole region of Northeast Africa, and the so called "Middle East" were black. In addition to the black complexion of the Israelites, another feature of the Israelites was their distinct full beards. Hashem gave an order to the men of Israel to not shave the beards, nor round the corners of the head[44].

When you consider the Talmudic tradition of the descriptions of the sons of Noah, and you also consider what is written in the book of Leviticus, it is quite clear that during the years circa 1400 BC, the description of the Israelites was that of a melanated black people, with the men having full beards. The mixed multitude of people amongst the Israelites were a black, smooth faced people.

---

[44] KJV Bible Leviticus 19:27

NUMBERS

During the years circa 1410-1400 BC, Hashem ordered Israel to be numbered. By the time Israel was ordered to be numbered, laws were already established pertaining to how to identify white affliction in their skin. Israel had laws on how to interact, and how to deal with white affliction in their skin. White complexion at this time in history was still viewed as something unclean, and certainly was not the complexion of the Israelites, or the Egyptians.

The Israelites were black at this time in history, and they procreated, commingled, and cohabitated with the mixed multitude of Egyptians. This occurred before crossing over Jordan and entering into the land of Canaan. Upon dealing with the mixed multitude within the camps, Hashem made it clear to Moses within his law that was being given to the Israelites, that if anyone had white complexion or white spots on them, they were considered unclean and had to be placed without the camp[45].

White complexion was not something that was common, or accepted within the house of Israel. In the 12th chapter of Numbers, there is a very telling incident that occurred amongst the siblings of Moses. Miriam, the sister of Moses, and Aaron was cursed with white complexion, because she was upset that Moses married a non-Israelite, a black Cushite woman.

The Torah passage reads as follows:

"And Miriam and Aaron spake against Moses because of the Ethiopian woman whom he had married: for he had married an Ethiopian woman. 2 And they said, Hath the Lord indeed spoken only by Moses? And the Lord Heard it. 3 (Now the man Moses was very meek, above all the men which were upon the earth.) 4 And the Lord spake suddenly unto Moses, and unto Aaron, and unto Miriam, COME OUT YE THREE UNTO THE TABERNACLE OF THE CONGREGATION. And they came out. 5 And the Lord came down in the pillar of the cloud, and stood in the door of the tabernacle, and called Aaron and Miriam: and they both came forth. 66 And he said,

---

[45] KJV Bible Numbers 5:1-2

HEAR NOW MY WORDS: IF THERE BE A PROPHET AMONG YOU, I THE LORD WILL MAKE MYSELF KNOWN UNTO HIM IN A VISION, AND WILL SPEAK UNTO HIM IN A DREAM. 7 MY SERVANT MOSES IS NOT SO, WHO IS FAITHFUL IN ALL MINE HOUSE. 8 WITH HIM I SPEAK MOUTH TO MOUTH, EVEN APPARENTLY, AND NOT IN DARK SPEECHES; AND THE SIMILITUDE OF THE LORD SHALL HE BEHOLD: WHEREFORE THEN WERE YE NOT AFRAID TO SPEAK AGAINST MY SERVANT MOSES? 9 And the anger of the Lord was kindled against them; and he departed. And the cloud departed from off the tabernacle; and, behold, Mariam became leprous, white as snow: and Aaron looked upon Miriam, and, behold, she was leprous. 11 And Aaron said unto Moses, Alas, my lord, I beseech thee, lay not the sin upon us, wherein we have done foolishly, and wherein we have sinned. 12 Let her not be as one dead, of whom the flesh is half consumed when he cometh out of the mother's womb"[46]

In this passage, it is evident that the Israelites did not view white complexion favorably. When Hashem was upset with Miriam, he cursed her with white complexion. Aaron pleaded with Moses not to lay this sin upon his sister Miriam. In fact, he doubled down on his fear, and dread for white complexion, by referring to it as something dead, or half consumed, coming out of the womb. The passage is a clear indicator that after the Exodus, and during the time in the wilderness, the Israelites were certainly unfamiliar with white complexion. They believed this complexion to be synonymous with a curse, sin, and death. Moses pleaded with Hashem to return her color back to her.

Hashem obliged, and her color returned after 7 days had passed. This is the proper amount of time for someone with the curse of leprosy, which is white complexion, to be put away until they are clean/healed, and their natural complexion returned. These people viewed white complexion as something foreign to them, and certainly nothing that they desired or wanted to be a part of. In this passage, it is obvious that Miriam's complexion was not white, because Hashem returned her skin to the black complexion that it was previously.

When you examine the Talmudic tradition, and remain mindful while reading the Torah, the evidence is irrefutable regarding the complexion of

---

[46] KJV Bible Numbers 12:1-12

the Israelites. There is no doubt that during the years circa 1410-1400 BC, The Israelites were a black nation, and they procreated, commingled, and were cohabiting with the black complexioned, mixed multitude of Egyptians. This was done with the other nations before crossing over Jordan, and entering into the land of Canaan.

DEUTERONOMY

During the years circa 1410-1400 BC, when the gift and a curse was given to the children of Israel on Mount Horeb, they were still a black Nation. The Israelites were given very clear injunctions on how to govern themselves, and were told to cleave to, and obey, the law that was revealed to them by Moses.

G-D lays out in this book of the law, the benefits of obedience to him. The Holy One, blessed be HE, also made clear the consequences of failing to obey Him; warning that disobedience to HIM would have grave consequences. One of the consequences described to the children of Israel is that they will be banished from the land of Canaan, and removed into other nations by ships[47].

The passage reads as follows:

"And the Lord will bring you into Egypt again with ships, by the way whereof I have spoken, Thou shall see it no more again: and there ye shall be sold unto your enemies for bondmen and bond women, and no man shall buy you"[48]

It is important to note here that this verse from Hashem is talking about a future prophecy against Israel. Israel was already in the midst of their exodus from Egypt. There is no way this verse was talking about the Israelites' time in Egypt, for that time had passed by the time of this prophecy. The collateral damage for the Israelites would be that they would lose their identity, and the memory of them would cease from amongst men[49]. The passage reads as follows:

---

[47] KJV Bible Deuteronomy 28:68

[48] ibid

[49] KJV Bible Deuteronomy 32:26

"I SAID I WILL SCATTER THEM INTO CORNERS, I WILL MAKE THE REMEMBRANCE OF THEM TO CEASE FROM AMONG MEN"[50]. Today we see that this prophecy from G-D has most certainly come to pass seeing that there is a whole nation of Japhetic, white complexioned people who claim to be the bloodline Israelites identified in the Torah. Clarification of the racial identity of the bloodline Israelites is necessary, because there are masses of people, within various nations, who erroneously believe that the bloodline Israelites were always a white complexioned people. Well, now, they can be set free from this lie, and govern themselves accordingly by properly making amends to the very people that they have disregarded, and mistreated, within these various nations.

Concerning the white complexioned, gentile people, who claim that they were always the people of the Torah, this verse is proof that this relative truth, to them, is a false truth in reality. Again, G-D stated that the Identity of the Israelites would be lost amongst men, which literally means that the inhabitants of the earth would forget who the bloodline Israelites are. Unfortunately, the masses of people have undergone a forced indoctrination to believe in an alternative narrative of the biblical Israelites. They have had to accept this false truth as reality for the last 200 years, and most certainly at the advent of cinematic distribution.

The book of Deuteronomy is replete with future prophecy regarding the bloodline Israelites, and what will befall them if they were disobedient to the law given to them from G-D, through Moses. These prophecies spake of them being exiled from the land of Canaan, and scattered to the 4 corners of the earth. These prophecies also spoke of the wickedness, and terror they would experience during their diaspora to the corners of the earth. G-D was very clear in Deuteronomy 28, verses 15-68, that the Israelites would suffer unimaginable horror for a specified period of time.

[50] ibid

After reading this passage, you will find prophecy of the horrors of the Israelites being subjected to slavery, being hanged from trees, and their children being violently taken away from them, and going into bondage. You will also find in this passage that they would certainly build a nation that they will never prosper in, that their women, and men would be raped, that they would have no assurance of their lives. Ultimately there would be no power in their hands to defend themselves against these horrors. This passage also prophesies that the religion that the Israelites would be given during these times will be a false religion, and something other than what was given to them from the G-D of Abraham.

When you read this passage, You will find in prophecies stating that the Israelites will have yokes of irons placed on their necks until they are completely broken in spirit, and until they surrender to a false god, within a false and foreign faith. In addition to these things, you will also find that these spiritually broken Israelites will serve these nations in nakedness, with a bloodthirsty lust for consumption, and that they will be hated by all nations, and called a byword wherever they be found. Lastly, you will find that this passage identifies this foreign nation as a nation that their forefathers have never known, and that they will be a particularly wicked nation. Their language would be foreign, and that their distinct character of cruelty will show no mercy for the elderly, or for babies.

It is important to remember, and consider, that Hashem was giving this prophecy exclusively to a deeply melanated, afro-asiatic black nation of people. During the years circa 1410-1400 BC, The Israelites were given two paths to consider, that would ultimately determine the fate of their nation. In this book of the law, Deuteronomy 30, verse 19, reads as follows:

I call heaven and earth to record this day against you, that I have set before you life and death, blessing and cursing: therefore choose life, that both thou and thy seed may live: 20 That thou mayest love the Lord thy G-D, and that thou mayest cleave unto him: for he is thy life, and the length of thy

days: that thou mayest dwell in the land which the Lord swore unto thy fa-
thers, to Abraham, to Isaac, and to Jacob, to give to them[51]".

The Israelites were indeed given the choice to be obedient to Hashem, but they ultimately chose to be disobedient. This disobedience fulfilled another prophecy in Deuteronomy 31, verses 16-18. This passage reads as follows:

"And the Lord said unto Moses, BEHOLD, THOU SHALT SLEEP WITH THY FA-THERS; AND THIS PEOPLE WILL RISE UP, AND GO WHORING AFTER THE GODS OF THE STRANGERS OF THE LAND, WHITHER THEY GO TO BE AMONG THEM, AND WILL FOR-SAKE ME, AND BREAK MY COVENANT WHICH I HAVE MADE WITH THEM. 17 THEN MY ANGER SHALL BE KINDLED AGAINST THEM IN THAT DAY, AND I WILL FORSAKE THEM, AND I WILL HIDE MY FACE FROM THEM, AND THEY SHALL BE DEVOURED, AND MANY EVILS AND TROUBLES SHALL BEFALL THEM; SO THAT THEY WILL SAY IN THAT DAY, ARE NOT THESE EVILS COME UPON US, BECAUSE OUR G-D IS NOT AMONG US? 18 AND I WILL SURELY HIDE MY FACE IN THAT DAY FOR ALL THE EVILS WHICH THEY SHALL HAVE WROUGHT, IN THAT THEY TURNED UNTO OTHER GODS[52]"

These future prophecies of curses that would befall the Israelites mentioned in this chapter, were told to the Israelite nation who were a black complexioned people. Before summarizing the book of Deuteronomy, I want to quickly examine another critically important prophecy that for whatever reason, seems to be overlooked amongst those who claim to adhere to the Abrahamic faith. In this book of the law, Hashem is seething with anger at the disobedience of his people.

In his anger, Hashem says:

"20 And he said, I WILL HIDE MY FACE FROM THEM, I WILL SEE WHAT THEIR END SHALL BE: FOR THEY ARE A VERY FROWARD GENERATION, CHILDREN IN WHOM IS NO FAITH. 21 THEY HAVE PROVOKE ME TO JEALOUSY WITH THAT WHICH IS NOT G-D; THEY HAVE PROVOKED ME TO ANGER WITH THEIR VANITIES: AND I WILL MOVE

---

[51] KJV Bible Deuteronomy 30:19-20

[52] KJV Bible Deuteronomy 31:16-18

THEM TO JEALOUSY WITH THOSE WHICH ARE NOT A PEOPLE; I WILL PROVOKE THEM TO ANGER WITH A FOOLISH NATION"[53].

There is an awful lot to unpack in this prophetic statement from G-D, but there are two major points:

- The first point Is that any form of spiritual practice that the Israelites would follow that is not found in the Torah is NOT a spiritual practice that is acceptable to the G-D of Abraham, Isaac, and Jacob. It is abundantly clear that such deviation from Torah, angers G-D. Hashem prophesied that his people have provoked, and will provoke him to anger in the future by worshiping everything other than what he has prescribed for them.
- The second point is that as a result of this jealousy, G-D feels he will in turn cause the Israelites to experience this same feeling, by using people who are not his people. These people will receive some of the benefits and provisions he had set aside for his people. G-D also said that he will provoke his people to anger with a foolish nation. This ultimately means that there will be a nation that is hell bent on causing the Israelites misfortune at every opportunity.

For the sake of clarification, the G-D of Abraham was provoked to jealousy, and he prophesied that he will cause the Israelites to experience this same feeling by blessing another nation. What this means, is that In order for this prophecy to be fulfilled, there must be a people in close proximity to the Israelites in the diaspora, that G-D will give some of his favor in their endeavors, that would cause his downtrodden people to be jealous. This prophecy is not fulfilled by a people who simply may have a financial advantage over his people, for some of his people in the diaspora by virtue of being who they are, will find a way to acquire finances. No, this prophecy is

---

[53] KJV Bible Deuteronomy 32: 20-21

only fulfilled if there is a nation of people, who as a result of his favor, who then would claim to be his people altogether.

It is this precise feeling of jealousy that G-D felt, when his people were giving praise to deities that were not him. It is also the exact feeling that he feels when his people, today, are worshiping false gods, and are giving praise to deities within these so called new found spiritual faiths; faiths, and gods that Abraham, Isaac, and Jacob never knew. This prophecy is fully complete when these things occur within a nation of foolish people that provokes the Israelites to anger by oppressing them at every opportunity. In order for a prophecy of this magnitude to materialize, there would need to be a gentile people, within a wicked nation, that will make a concerted effort to literally erase the image and likeness of the Israelites, and masquerade around themselves as the bloodline Israelites. For a whole nation of people to have their true identity forgotten, it truly takes a wicked and foolish nation to go above and beyond to suppress this information.

To summarize the book of Deuteronomy, and to end the reexamination of the Torah, in the years circa 1410-1400 BC the biblical Israelites were a Afro-asiatic black complexioned people. They were given the choice of being blessed, or cursed from their G-D. It was prophesied that the Israelites would ultimately choose the latter of the choices, which would gradually in time lead to them being a pillaged, and subjugated nation of people. Their true identity would be lost amongst men. It is prophesied in the Torah that Israel would ultimately be a hated nation upon the earth. The main nation to whom the Israelites would find themselves subjected to in their future prophecy, was a nation of people their forefathers never knew. This completely rules out Esau, and his progeny of Edomites.

The patriarchs, and matriarchs of the Israelites knew Esau, therefore, it is impossible for the white people who participated, and are currently participating in the prophesied subjugation of the Israelites in the diaspora, to be a nation of Edomites. The Torah makes clear that any nation that the Israelites were scattered into was a nation that was clearly unknown to Abraham,

33

Isaac, and Jacob. Ultimately, from the time of Abraham, up until the years circa 1400 BC, the Israelites never interacted with, or knew any Japhetic nation.

NEVI'IM

When analyzing the Nevi'im, what will be addressed are the most popular verses that reference the complexion of the Israelites. It is important to provide a timeline of when these passages were written. This is to ensure that the physical descriptions of Israelites remain consistent throughout the writings of the prophets. This process is necessary so that their complexion is somehow not lost upon the reader. At this point, it is already established via Torah, and Talmud, that the Semitic(of Shem) people were black. What's more important to remember is the Israelites were a black complexioned people, who were often mistaken for Egyptians.

There was a significant amount of time that had passed between the death of Joshua, and the reign of king Saul within the land of Canaan. During that time, when Israel was without a king, there was little admixing between the Israelites and the Hamitic nations. Also during this time, there was very little procreating with other Semitic nations. It was approximately 350-400 years that had passed when the nation of Israel was ruled by Judges.

This time frame begins from the death of Joshua, and concludes at the appointing of King Saul. This period was effectively called the time of the Judges. Israel was without a king until the years circa 1050 BC, when Samuel, the priest anointed king Saul. Some believe that it was during this time of the judges that Israel procreated with various nations, and somehow became a white complexioned nation. As a result, some people attempt to identify king Davids' complexion as "fair". Some have been erroneously interpreting "fair" to mean white, or even light complexioned for a very long time.

To further illustrate the impossibility for a whole nation of people to change complexions over a 400 year period, I will draw upon:

(1) the parallels between the Negroes timeline in America from 1619-2020.
(2) and that of the black complexioned Israelites timeline from 1410-1050 BC, after they entered the land of Canaan, when they would eventually live an extended period without a king.

In America in 1619, there were more white people than Negroes. There were laws in place that prohibited whites from procreating with Negroes[54] albeit enslaved, or free. Over the course of the last 400 years, and even with a minority of Negroes procreating with other ethnic populations in America, the Negro remains black. The Negro complexion in America has not changed in the last 400 years.

The Torah was in the possession of the Israelites, and they had a law that prohibited procreation with other nations. Therefore, the Israelites' complexion in the land of Cannan did not change either. This is an indictment against anyone who would even fancy, or concoct such a silly idea, that during this approximately 400 year time period, the complexion of the Israelites could have been whitened. The nations surrounding Israel, both Hamitic, and Semitic, were black complexioned people.

To put it plainly, if the Negro complexion did not turn white after 400 years of being surrounded by whites, being enslaved and raped by whites, and being unmercifully subjugated by whites in America, then, there is no chance that the Israelites complexion would turn white when they were completely surrounded by black nations. In addition to this, Israel had extended periods of peace as a result of actually following the laws that were given to them which amongst many, included the prohibition on procreating with not only white people, but other black nations.

To clear up any confusion surrounding King David's complexion, you have to remember that Ruth was a Moabite who procreated with an Israelite which ultimately led to king David. According to Rabbinical tradition, Shem was black complexioned, and so was Terah, the father of Abraham, Nahor,

---

[54] British Colonial Law 1664

and Haran. Haran is the father of Lot, who is the father of Moab. We know for certain that the Moabites did not have the prohibition on procreating with any other nations, so it is almost a certainty that they procreated with other Hamitic nations.

The Moabites were completely surrounded by black Hamitic nations, as well as other black Semitic nations. The Moabites were not in close proximity to any of the white Japhetic nations. Ruth was black complexioned, and the grandmother of king David, and the Israelites were a deeply melanated black people from their birth, circa 1930 BC. They remained that way throughout the approximately 1000 years even unto the reign of king Saul circa 1050 BC.

When describing king David, his cheeks were described as being ruddy, and his countenance as very pleasant to look upon[55]. This term ruddy was also used to describe Esau, who was the son of two black complexioned Semitic people. David had a brownish red hue to him, and the Nevi'im interestingly says that Goliath disdained him because he was young, ruddy(brownish red), and handsome[56]. This disdain for David's complexion was a byproduct of Goliath being white complexioned.

Previously established, the fallen angels were described as being white, and we know that the giants were the seed of fallen angels. Goliath was a direct seed of Og, who was the king of the Bashan. Og was a giant, the seed of a fallen angel, and his complexion was white. One can conclude that he had to have procreated with some Philistines at some point in order to spread his white complexioned, giant, dna amongst some of them. It should be noted that not all the Philistines were white, but a specific lineage amongst them were. Not all the Philistines were giants, and it is because of this reality, one can further conclude, and know for sure, that the majority of

---

[55] KJV Bible 1Samuel 16:12

[56] KJV Bible 1Samuel 17:42

the Hamitic Philistines remained black, even after admixing with the white descendants of the former king Og.

In the years circa 1011-1000 BC, David became King of Israel, and unified the northern and southern kingdoms. The women who married King David were black complexioned, Semitic women. After 40 years of reigning in Israel by King David, Solomon became King in the years circa 971 BC. Nevi'im records King Solomon as having many wives. The most prominent amongst them were Naamah, Pharaoh's daughter, and the Queen of Sheba Makeda. Both were black complexioned, Hamitic women.

Though the book of Songs of Solomon is allegorical, there are some key words used in the book that causes controversy concerning the complexions of Solomon, and his beloved Shulamite woman. Because these verses are in the Tanakh, I will briefly address them. In the Song of Solomon, the bride is speaking about her beloved, and she describes herself as being black complexioned, and comely[57]. Comely being interpreted as very pleasing, and/or "fair"[58]. The verse reads as follows:

"I am black, but comely, O ye daughters of Jerusalem, as the tents of Kedar, as the curtains of Solomon. 6 Look not upon me because I am black, because the sun hath looked upon me; my mothers children were angry with me; they made me the keeper of the vineyards; but mine own vineyard have I not kept[59]".

For those who interpret this verse literally, this verse is very telling regarding the complexion of the Shulamite woman. This verse is then understood that this woman was a black woman surrounded by black Semitic, and Hamitic peoples. Again, as stated earlier, the vast majority of these people

---

[57] KJV Bible Song of Solomon 1:5

[58] Ibid 1:6

[59] Ibid

were black complexioned. The white descendants of Japheth, had yet, to enlarge themselves amongst the Semitic peoples.

There is another verse in the book of the Song of Solomon, that those who interpret the verse literally, use as evidence that is very clear regarding the black complexion of Solomon. The verse reads as follows:

"My Beloved is white and ruddy, the chiefest among ten thousand. 11 His head is as the most fine gold, his locks are bushy, and black as a raven[60].

It is important to clarify that the word "white" does not appear in this verse in the Hebrew script. A more accurate translation of this would have been: "my beloved is without blemish and ruddy, the chiefest among ten thousand". Here, one can read this in the Hebrew:

Song of Songs 5 ⌄   ☆   אA

10. דּוֹדִי צַח וְאָדוֹם דָּגוּל מֵרְבָבָה:

My beloved is clear-skinned and ruddy, Preeminent among ten thousand.

61

Again, In this verse, the Hebrew word for white (לבן) is simply not there.

To bring full clarity to the term red/ruddy, and end the possibility that it is referring to white complexion in any way, red/ruddy will be clearly defined in Hebrew. The Hebrew word for red is אדום. Here are two passages in the Torah where this term is used to describe Esau, and the sacrificial heifer/ cow. In Genesis 25:25 Esau is described as אדום in this passage;

---

[60] KJV Bible Song of Solomon 5:10-11

[61] Song of Songs 5:10

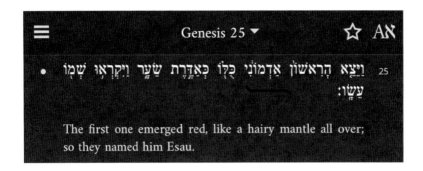

25 וַיֵּצֵא הָרִאשׁוֹן אַדְמוֹנִי כֻּלּוֹ כְּאַדֶּרֶת שֵׂעָר וַיִּקְרְאוּ שְׁמוֹ
עֵשָׂו:

The first one emerged red, like a hairy mantle all over;
so they named him Esau.

The verse is clearly describing his complexion as being red and hairy.

And in the book of Numbers 19, verse 2, אדמה being used to describe the heifer that is acceptable for sacrifice unto G-D.

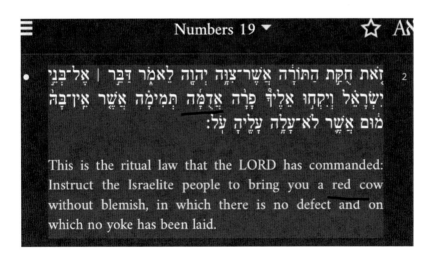

2 זֹאת חֻקַּת הַתּוֹרָה אֲשֶׁר־צִוָּה יְהוָה לֵאמֹר דַּבֵּר | אֶל־בְּנֵי
יִשְׂרָאֵל וְיִקְחוּ אֵלֶיךָ פָרָה אֲדֻמָּה תְּמִימָה אֲשֶׁר אֵין־בָּהּ
מוּם אֲשֶׁר לֹא־עָלָה עָלֶיהָ עֹל:

This is the ritual law that the LORD has commanded:
Instruct the Israelite people to bring you a red cow
without blemish, in which there is no defect and on
which no yoke has been laid.

Here is an image of a red cow/פרה אדמה

62

We can clearly see from these images that Esau was a black man with a reddish/brown hue to him. Since this is the same word used describing King David, and King Solomon, then, certainly when David procreated with other black Semitic women, his children were black. When Solomon procreated with both Namaah, and Makeda, his progeny most certainly were very dark complexioned by virtue of them being Hamitic women. To put it plainly, during the years circa 971-931 BC, when the kingdom was divided into north(Israel), and south(Judah), the Israelites were a black complexioned people who were surrounded by black Hamitic peoples.

---

62 iStock image search for פרה אדומה

In the years circa 722 BC, the northern kingdom of Israel was conquered and taken captive into the land of Assyria. The northern kingdom consisted of the 10 northern tribes of Israel, they were taken and never returned to the land of Israel[63]. It is important to emphasize that the Assyrian's were a black complexioned, Semitic people during these years, so any possible assimilating into this group of people wouldn't affect the complexion of the Israelites. It is at this point, the possibility exists, that a small percentage of the northern 10 tribes of Israel could have been exiled into the Japhetic nations.

Though it is almost a certainty that some of the northern 10 tribes of Israel were taken into the Japhetic(European) nations, it would've been a minority of people from the tribes. According to Rabbinical tradition, Sennacherib, the king of Assyria, banished the 10 northern tribes of Israel into Africa. The Talmud reads as follows:

Sanhedrin 94a ▼

The William Davidson Talmud

☆ אא

≡

15 להיכא אגלי להו מר זוטרא אמר לאפריקי ורבי חנינא
אמר להרי סלוג אבל ישראל ספרו בגנותה של ארץ
ישראל כי מטו שוש אמרי שויא כי ארעין כי מטו
עלמין אמרו כעלמין כי מטו שוש תרי אמרי על חד
תרין

The Gemara asks: **To where did** Sennacherib **exile the** ten tribes? **Mar Zutra says:** He exiled them **to Afrikei, and Rabbi Ḥanina says: To the Selug Mountains.** The Gemara adds: **But** those exiled from the kingdom of **Israel spoke in disparagement of Eretz Yisrael** and extolled the land of their exile. **When they arrived** at one place, they called it **Shosh,** as **they said: It is equal [shaveh] to our land. When they arrived** at another place, they called it **Almin,** as **they said: It is like our world [almin],** as Eretz Yisrael is also called *beit olamim.* **When they arrived** at a third place they called it **Shosh the second [terei],** as **they said: For one** measure of good in Eretz Yisrael, there are **two [terein]** here.

---

[63] KJV Bible 2 Kings 17:6-23

This passage from the Talmud actually supports the prophecy of Zephaniah.

The book of Zephaniah reads as follows:

"FROM BEYOND THE RIVERS OF ETHIOPIA MY SUPPLIANTS, EVEN THE DAUGHTER OF MY DISPERSED, SHALL BRING MINE OFFERING[64]".

G-D, through the prophet Zephania, places the dispersed or "lost" tribes of Israel in Africa, and more specifically, from the other side of Cush/Ethiopia, which is west Africa. In the years circa 722-640 BC, Israel yet remained a black complexioned people, with a remnant of the northern tribes being exiled within the white complexioned Japhetic nations.

During the years circa 605 BC, the southern kingdom of Judah is conquered by the Babylonian Empire[65], and they would remain there for 70 years. The Israelites were surrounded by other black complexioned Hamitic, and Semitic people during this exile. Though Israel would endure another long period of subjugation at the hands of another empire, their black complexion did not change, in fact, it was described as getting darker due to their calamities. The prophet Jeremiah laments the conditions of the Judaens, and is filled with sorrow when he cries out to G-D. The lamentation of Jeremiah is recorded in the book of Lamentations. The passage read as follows:

"Their visage is blacker than a coal; they are not known in the streets: their skin cleaveth to their bones; it is withered, it is become like a stick"[66]. The prophet Jeremiah then doubles down on how the Judeans complexion had gotten darker because of their suffering, when he said, "Our skin was black like an oven because of the terrible famine"[67].

---

64 KJV Bible Zephaniah 3:10

65 KJV Bible 2 Kings 24:1-7

66 KJV Bible Lamentations 4:8

67 KJV Bible Lamentations 5:10

After the 70 years in captivity that ended in the years circa 538 BC[68], Cyrus, the Persian King, defeats the Babylonians, and issues a decree allowing the Judeans to return back to Israel. Israel was still a black complexioned nation upon their return. As demonstrated earlier, it would be very difficult for the Israelites' complexion to change over the 70 years of being exiled in another black complexioned nation.

It is during the years circa 480-470 BC, that one begins to see Israel surrounded by Japhetic nations. The prophetess Esther, married the Persian king Ahasuerus, and helped preserve the lives of the remnant of Israelites that remained in Persian Exile. Though the Israelites were beginning to be surrounded by some Japhetic people, there is no evidence that their complexion changed during this time.

From the years circa 330 BC, until 70 AD, the land of Israel was occupied by Japhetic nations. It was during the years circa 165 BC, when Judas Maccabaeus fought against the Japhetic, enemy nations of Israel. We have already established that the Japhetic nations were a white complexioned people, and Judas Maccabeus clearly identifies them as having a likeness, or image other than the Israelites.

In the Apocryphal writings, 1 Maccabees 3:48 reads as follows:
"And Laid open the book of the law, wherein the heathen had sought to paint the likeness of their images"
After fighting against these Japhetic nations, and attempting to rededicate their temple, it is clear that procreating with these nations was not a priority. Israel yet remained a black nation up until the destruction of the Temple in the year circa 70 AD.

---

[68] A Timeline of Biblical History

DIASPORA

After the destruction of the temple in the year 70 AD, the Romans killed many Israelites, and those that survived, they sold into slavery. There was a strong presence of black Israelites in the city of Cyrene, Libya who led a successful revolt, and fought against the Romans, in the year circa 117-125 AD[69]. This war has been referred to by historians as the Kitos War. It is recorded that the Israelites killed over 100 thousand Romans, and completely pushed them out of northern Libya. As a result of this victory against the Romans, the Israelites were able to attempt to establish a Sanhedrin in Cyrene.

In the years Circa 132-136 AD, the black Israelites again fought against Roman forces in Israel. During this engagement with the Romans, the Israelites again killed over 100 thousand of their soldiers, causing them to retreat from the land of Israel. This revolt against the Romans has been called the Bar Kokhba Revolt by Historians. This was the last strong fight against the Romans that Israel would put up before the state of Israel would be completely destroyed. After Israel put up the fight against the Romans, taking back many cities, a Sanhedrin was re-established within Judea. Roman Emperor, Hadrian, sent Julius Severus, and Hadrianus Urbicus to finally put an end to the Jewish state. The survivors were sold into slavery in other Roman territories in Europe, and into northern Africa, including Egypt[70]. It is at this time, the name of Judea, was changed to Palestine.

During the Years circa 175-219 CE, Israel still remained a black complexioned nation that was subjected to religious persecution, and harsh cruelties in all of the territories under Roman rule. It was during these times it became important for the Israelites to start putting into writing the Oral Torah,

---

[69] "Dio's Rome, Volume V., Book 68, paragraph 32"

[70] Ancient Jewish History: The Bar-Kokhba Revolt, Jewish Virtual Library

also called Mishna. Otherwise, it could get lost forever under their duress during their diaspora. At this time, the Romans had a copy of the Torah. The only thing that separated the bloodline Israelites from the other heathen nations that had a copy of the Torah, was the Mishna. It was of great importance to, by any means necessary, secretly put into writing the Mishna, so that it could be shared by the bloodline Israelites.

The black complexioned Israelites completed the Jerusalem Talmud in the years circa 290 AD. In The years circa 370 AD, Rabbana Ashi Ben Simai built schools of learning for Torah, and Mishna, in the city of Sura in Babylon. He presided over these institutions of learning for 50 years in Babylon, until the years circa 420 AD. Rabbi Mar- Zutra, and Rabbi Mar-Kahana were contemporaries of Rabbana Ashi. They were all black complexioned, masters of the written Torah, and Mishna.

To stress the importance of the Mishna, and why it is, and was so important for the Israelites to learn, I will share a poem expressed during the years of the 3 Rabbi's mentioned above. "Moses requested permission to commit to writing the Mishna or Oral Law, but G-D saw in advance that the nations would one day possess a Greek translation of Torah, and would affirm: 'We are Israel; we are the children of G-D,' while the Jewish people would also declare, 'We are G-D's children,' and He therefore gave a token for this purpose: 'He who possesses my secret (mysterion) is my son.' This secret is the Mishna and the oral exegesis of the Law. Therefore did the prophet Hosea say: "Were I to write the fullness of the Law, Israel would be accounted as a stranger[71].'"

With the perspective of the Mishna being the spiritual element that separates the black complexioned, bloodline Israelites from the white complexioned Japhetic nations, the other black complexioned Semitic nations, and Hamitic nations, the dispersed Israelites completed the Talmud in Baby-

---

[71] History of the Jews: by Professor H. Graetz VOL. II pg. 608

lonia during the years circa 425-470 AD. They would teach the Mishna in the academies they set up, to other Israelites, imploring them to cleave to it, and to master it while they were yet under subjugation in Babylon. During the years circa 490 AD, there was a significant wave of Israelites that migrated to the Malabar coast of India, fleeing the persecution they were enduring in Babylonia[72].

In the years circa 640 AD, there was a large Israelite community in Libya. These Israelites were led by Queen Diyah Kahina, who organized and defeated both Roman forces, and Arab forces in North Africa[73]. Those Israelites that fled into Africa from persecution yet remained after defeating the Romans previously in 125 AD. It is important to note that the Israelites were routinely successful in their defending of Libya against the Arabs until the death of Queen Kahina Circa 705 AD. After her death, many of the Israelites began to embrace and convert to Islam. Though the Israelites began to expand in their faith, they yet remained a black complexioned nation of people.

In the years circa 800 AD, Eldad Ha-Dani presented stories of having lived amongst the tribes of Reuben, Issachar, Zebulun, Ephraim, Manasseh, and Simeon in his travels. Eldad Ha-Dani said that he lived amongst the tribes of Dan, Naphtali, Gad, and Aasher in Africa[74]. The black complexioned Israelites in Tunisia received his narrative, and believed him to be truthful[75]. Eldad Ha-Dani expounded upon his experiences amongst the Israelites in Africa, stating that they had sitting kings, and a full Sanhedrin in Africa. The Israelites in Tunisia that he returned to tell of his experiences during his trav-

---

[72] Ibid pg 630

[73] Ancient History Encyclopedia: Kahina

[74] The Ritual of Eldad Ha-Dani: Reconstructed and Edited From Manuscripts and a Genizah

[75] Jewish History: Chabad.org Eldad Ha-Dani

els had been there for almost 1000 years, dating back to the northern tribes being taken into Assyrian captivity.

The land of Khazaria, prior to the years of their conversion to the faith of the Hebrews circa 740 AD, was a land friendly to exiles from other lands. Some Israelites who remained subjugated under Byzantium rule, fled to Khazaria because of their tolerance of the Hebrews[76]. Yes, there were black complexioned Israelites who entered into the land of Khazaria and procreated with some of the people, creating a specific line of people who can legitimately say they are bloodline Israelites. It was the King, his attendants, and the ruling class that converted, and became Jews[77]. Again, it was only a specific group of people that had procreated with the Israelites. It was a royal class of people who embraced the Hebrew Faith, these were the leaders, members of the upper class, and the kings who became "Jewish"[78]. King Bulan adopted the Rabbinical form of the Hebrew Faith, instead of the Karaite form, which means he was definitely taught by black complexioned Israelites. At that time, the black complexioned Israelites were the only transmitters of the Mishna.

From the 11th century through the 13th century, the majority of the tribes of Israel resided throughout Africa, with a remnant of them residing in India, Arabia, Babylon, Spain, Khazaria, Rome, Greece, Iran, and Portugal. During these years, the Israelites were still a black complexioned people, even though some of them were surrounded by the white complexioned Japhetic nations in Europe. While living in exile in these Japhetic nations, the laws regarding conversion to the Hebrew Faith yet remained. It is more than a certainty that some of the peoples within the Japhetic nations converted to the Hebrew Faith during these years. The Israelites who were in Africa were

---

[76] The Thirteenth Tribe: Arthur Koestler.

[77] Ibid pg 60

[78] The Jews of Khazaria: Keven Alan Brook. Pg 21.

48

surrounded by other black Semitic and Hamitic peoples. The same laws of conversion applied to these people also. This circumstance would remain the same up until the Spanish Inquisition of the 1400's.

INQUISITION

Though there were many inquisitions that had taken place amongst the Japhetic nations against the Israelites, I want to primarily focus on the Spanish Inquisition of 1478, and that of Portugal in 1536. During the writing of this book, up until this point, I have been careful to remind the reader of the complexion of the Israelites, so that at no point during the reading of this book, one could begin to believe that the Israelites complexion was anything other than black. Here are primary source writings, and paintings that will beyond a shadow of doubt, prove the complexion of the Israelites. These are descriptions presented by Japhetic nations, who most certainly knew who they were identifying.

Swedes, the Danes, the Brandenburghers, the North Ameri-
cans, and, fince 1778, with the Spaniards. Their trade however ftill increafed, not only by the Swedes and Brandenburghers
ceafing their navigations to the coaft of Guinea, but from the
annual demand of a fupply of more than 100,000 Negroe re-
cruits for their own colonies. The author confines his relation
of the firft Negroe-trade to that carried on by the Portuguefe
and Spaniards.

Gonzalez was the firft Portuguefe who, in 1442, returned with
Negroe flaves, purchafed; inftead of the Africans, who had, till
then, been carried off by mere violence. But foon after, the
Portuguefe became better acquainted with the African regions,
and their valuable productions. Prince Henry founded the firft
Guinea company; that fettled factories in the fortrefs of Arguin,
and got the exclufive privilege of trading with the Arabs. The
trade foon increafed; fo that, in 1455, not lefs than feven or eight
hundred Negroe flaves were annually exported to Lifbon. At
length the Portuguefe, in 1471, difcovered the Gold Coaft;
and ever fince, the intercourfe between Portugal and Guinea
was continued. The Portuguefe endeavoured to exclude other
nations from Guinea; whilft the reft of the European navigators
were, in fpite of papal bulls, and all the reports induftrioufly
fpread of the pretended dangers of that coaft, ftriving to get a
fhare of that profitable gold trade. The difcovery of the Gold
Coaft ferved, indeed, yet more to enlarge the fphere of the
navigation of the Portuguefe, than their flave-trade; but it
forced them alfo to extend themfelves on the coafts; and to
fettle colonies in Congo, Angola, and other places, which they
had till then neglected. Prince Henry's colonies were enlarged
by his fucceffors. King John II. in 1492, expelled all the Jews
to the ifland of St. Thomas, which had been difcovered in
1471, and to other Portuguefe fettlements on the continent of
Africa; and from thefe banifhed Jews, the black Portuguefe,
as they are called, and the Jews in Loango, who are defpifed
even by the very Negroes, are defcended. By thefe colonifts,
St. Thomas foon became a confiderable place of trade, and
valuable for its fugar plantations. Thirty years after their
fettlement, not lefs than one hundred and fifty-fix thoufand ar-
robes (of thirty pounds weight each) of fugar were exported;
and the engines of fixty fugar works, turned by flaves. Thefe
Negroes were purchafed in Guinea, Congo, and Manicongo, and
the colonifts had plantations furnifhed with from one hundred
and fifty to three thoufand Negroe flaves.

In the beginning of the fixteenth century, the Spaniards
and Portuguefe began to tranfport Negroes, for fimilar labours,
to the Weft Indies and Brafils, by which the Negroe trade was
rapidly increafed. The Spaniards, on their firft fettling in the
Weft Indies, immediately treated the natives of that part of the
globe according to the pope's inftruction; they divided them
by families or diftricts among themfelves, as flaves. The poor
In-

79 The Critical Review, Or, Annals Of Literature, Volume 57 Pg 141.

Indians were now forced to dive for pearls, to wash gold sand, and to work gold and silver mines for their new masters; they were often carried far from their native homes; and, in short, they were so miserably fed and used, that in a short time these countries were entirely depopulated. In order to supply that loss, the Spaniards carried off the other Indians, who were not yet subdued, by stratagem or force, especially from the Lucayan Islands. The Spanish court at last prohibited those violences; but the Spaniards soon found means for evading the orders of their court. They decried the Indians in Europe as the most sanguinary race of savages; on which Ferdinand repealed his former orders, and bade them carry off these cannibals by force from their native places, and to treat and sell them as slaves. With a great deal of pains and dangers, the Spaniards now carried away the number of labourers wanted for their exigencies, but soon found them too weak to support long and hard labours. Bishop Las Casas is generally thought to have been the first who advised the Spaniards to import slaves from Africa, in order to spare the Indians. But our author shews, that before that time, Moorish and even Negroe slaves were sent to America. Las Casas' merits consisted in saving South America from an entire depopulation: what before him had been already done by private Spanish individuals, he procured to be done by a general royal order, or he proposed Negroes instead of the few Moorish slaves, who had till then been sent to America. He also deserved well of the commerce of America, by procuring by his remonstrances, that the Negroe slaves, who before, like all other necessaries, had been sent from Seville, or other Spanish harbours, were to be directly transported from Guinea to the West Indies; and that, of course, America was more expeditiously furnished with the labourers wanted. Las Casas' proposal was executed in 1517. The court of trade at Seville appointed 4000 Negroes to be annually transported to the islands of Domingo, Fernandine, Porto Rico, and Jamaica; and Charles V. granted the monopoly of this slave-trade to his counsellor and major-domo de la Bresa for eight years, who, in his turn, sold his grant for that time to some Genoese, for 25000 ducats. The trade of these farmers probably ceased with the term of the eight years, as the Genoese sold their slaves too dear, and as the Portuguese were become very jealous of the trade of other nations to Guinea.

The number of slaves annually exported from Guinea now rose from year to year. Besides those wanted by the Portuguese for their own settlements in Africa, or sold by them to the Spaniards in the West Indies, great numbers of Negroes were also wanted for the Brasils, which had been lately discovered. The importance of that fruitful country, which for a long time remained a place of exile, was not known till about the middle of the sixteenth century. Some of its forced colonists had imitated

---

In this article, in 1492, King John II, expelled all the Jews out of Spain to the Island of St. Thomas, and to other Portuguese settlements in the continent of Africa. The article continues to inform us that the banished Jews were called the Black Portuguese. It also states that these black Jews that were kicked out of Spain, and the black Jews of the Loango, are despised even by the very Negroes from whom they are descended.

It further says that these Negroes were in Guinea, Congo, and Manicongo/Angola. In addition to this, the article says that these "Negroes" aka Jews, were transported to the West Indies and Brazil. To be very clear, the Jews who were kicked out of Spain, and Portugal were black complexioned people, who were sent to Puerto Rico, Jamaica, Dominica, the West Indies, and America. These Jews were called Negroes, and they were black complexioned people. This article further states that these "Negroes" (Jews) were very desirable because of their ability to cultivate lands where they inhabited.

The transporting of these black complexioned Israelites would only increase during the 15, and 1600's because the Dutch, and the French wanted to also make financial profits off of the enslavement of the black Israelites. These countries would at times go to war against one another for the purpose of benefiting the most off of the enslavement of the Israelites. One of the most famous incidents where these battling countries engaged one another was in 1619, when the Dutch intercepted a Portuguese vessel full of enslaved Negro Jews, and brought that ship to Virginia[81]. The arrival of these particular Israelites are remembered the most. However, Israelites were being transported to the Americas, and West Indies for at least a century prior.

What makes the state of Virginia significant in this conversation about the complexion of the Israelites, is that it is the only state that still has a

[81] Virginiaplaces.org: The Origins of Slavery in Virginia

monument that identifies the Israelites as Negroes. This Israel Hill monument speaks for itself when it highlights the accomplishments of these formerly enslaved Israelites, who formed a town to live in amongst themselves.

As mentioned earlier, the Jews began to migrate to Malabar, India, during the years circa 479 AD. 1000 years later, and the Portuguese are painting the Israelites as black complexioned people.

This picture was painted circa 1540 AD, and currently resides in a private library at the Biblioteca Casanatense in Rome.

File:Codice Casanatense Jews of Malabar.jpg

The picture below depicts Ethiopians, who were painted by the Portuguese at the same time as the paintings of the black complexioned Israelites. This collection of work was based off of the Portuguese's most frequent, and recent interactions[83] with the nations that they painted.

File:Codice Casanatense Ethiopians.jpg

☆ ✎

---

[83] Codice Casanatense info page.

In this photo below, the Portuguese painter illustrates that they were very familiar with the differences amongst the black complexioned nations when they painted the Nubians a darker complexion than the Israelites, and Ethiopians.

File:Codice Casanatense Nubians.jpg

The picture below illustrates that the Portuguese knew how to paint white images when appropriate. Here are a few photos that depict some Japhetic, Gentile nations. These photos were painted around the same time as the Negro paintings of the Israelites. These are the depictions of the Persians(male), and an Afghani(woman).

File:Codice Casanatense Shirazians.jpg

☆　　✎

This is a painting of Northern, and North-eastern Indian, men, as see through the eyes of the Portuguese.

File:Codice Casanatense Patanes.jpg

84

It is very clear at this point that the Spanish, and the Portuguese, knew exactly who they were dealing with, as illustrated through the painted differences of the nations. When the Spanish identified all the Jews that they kicked out of their country as Negroes, there is no doubt they knew the Negro Jews.

If the Spanish, or the Portuguese, identified the Jews as white, they would have painted them as such. They most certainly, would not have called them Negroes. To further prove how the other nations described and depicted the Israelites, on the next page, you will see photos housed in Russian Museums.

This is a photo of Israelites from the late 14th century in Russia.

85

85 Art Treasures of Russia: Harry N. Abrams, INC. Publishers New York

Another photo of how the Japhetic nations painted the Israelites in the early 15th century in Russia.

86

86 Art Treasures of Russia: Harry N. Abrams, INC. Publishers New York

The picture below illustrates that the Russians knew how to use white paint. Here is a recreated funeral scene that was painted in the late 15th century in Russia.

74. The Dormition of the Virgin
Embroidery. Late 15th century
Russian Museum, Leningrad

ints Worshiping the Virgin
idery. Late 15th century
n Museum, Leningrad

erpiece, both for the colorful execu-
lity of the lettered

In style close to icons of this period, this work follows
traditional iconography. Against a glory, Christ is lifting
Virgin's soul, represented by the figure of an infant. T
Virgin's soul, ding forward around the Virgin's body.
ints who have come to w [87]

---

[87] Art Treasures of Russia: Harry N. Abrams, INC. Publishers New York

Paintings of Israelites in 14th Century Moscow.

88

---

88 Art Treasures of Russia: Harry N. Abrams, INC. Publishers New York

A Greek painting from the 15th century of the Israelites. Surely the Grecians had first hand knowledge of the complexions of the Jews.

89

89 Art Treasures of Russia: Harry N. Abrams, INC. Publishers New York

Again, to illustrate that the Russians knew how to paint white images, these are the paintings of their likeness.

10 and 11. The Fathers of the church. *Mosaic. Cathedral of Hagia Sophia, Kiev. 10*

is Russia's springtime, the freshness of which is reflected in the purity and
f the art it produced. Severe ordeals and the nation's moral strength in meeting
ike reflected in the art of that time. This was the time when people saw more 90

---

90 Art Treasures of Russia: Harry N. Abrams, INC. Publishers New York

The evidence that has been presented so far in this book over-

whelmingly shows that the Biblical Israelites remained a predominantly black

complexioned nation from their birth, and throughout their diaspora.

CONCLUSION

It is fair to assume that the reader of this book may fancy him/herself as a believer of the Abrahamic Faith. If that is indeed the case, then the Torah, Mishna, Gemara, and the whole Tanakh is incumbent upon the believer to follow. For those of us who aspire to stand on every word of Hashem, that has been passed down to us by our forefathers, and sages of our Law, it is a certainty that identifying the complexion of the children of Israel will be very easy. Both, the Tanakh, and Mishna, are very clear about the complexion of the Israelites, and their ancestors.

The fact that the complexion of the bloodline Israelites is even a debate, or something that even needs clarity, illustrates that the word of Hashem is true. As stated earlier in this book, G-D said, because of the disobedience of the Israelites, that he will scatter them into the corners of the earth, and will cause the memory of Israel to cease from amongst men[91]. The saving grace to all of this is that Hashem also says, that when these things have befallen upon the Israelites, that if they turn to him Alone, and adhere to his Torah, that he will redeem them from all the curses that they brought upon themselves[92].

The Talmud states, that all of the progeny of Shem were black and beautiful (שחורים ונאים)[93], and if you follow the Tanakh, you will see that all the people they procreated with were black complexioned, Simitic, and Hamitic peoples. As stated earlier in the book, Esther married a Japhetic King, but marrying the King wouldn't, couldn't, and did not change the complexion of the bloodline Israelites. It is evidenced that the Israelites were

---

[91] Deuteronomy 32:26

[92] Ibid 30:1-9

[93] Talmud Pirkei DeRabbi Eliezer 24:1

scattered into other Japhetic nations, including Ashkenaz. Again, as stated earlier, it was King Bulan, and the upper class ruling family who converted to the faith of the Israelites[94].

The King is not the father of the whole nation. One can conclude that due to the King converting to the faith of the Israelites, others in his family, even if not only himself, procreated with some black complexioned Israelites. This therefore, creates a specific bloodline of people, who today, could pass as white complexioned Israelites. It is believed, and recorded throughout history, that Khazaria was a land that was tolerant of the Israelites[95]. One can reasonably conclude, the Israelites definitely procreated with some Khazarian converts, creating a specific line of bloodline Israelites. Today, we know that pretty much all the Khazarian, Ashkenazi people, claim to be bloodline Israelites. There is a standard that has been set, and has to be followed by them as well.

The standard is, just because King Bulan, and the royal families converted to the Rabbinical Faith of the Israelites, and procreated with some Israelites, does not mean that the whole nation are Israelites. This standard has been imposed upon the Israelites in Ethiopia. There are documented Kings written in the Tanakh (Menilek), whose bloodlines continue on to this day in Ethiopia(Hali Selassi). All Ethiopians are not considered Jews. Their Kings were, so how then can all the Ashkenazi be considered Jews? They can't be! The Israelites have always been, and will always be a predominantly black complexioned nation, with some black bloodline, white "passing" relatives within the Ashkenazi, and Sephardic communities.

It is because of the curses that the Israelites brought upon themselves, that the majority yet remain a pillaged people, still practicing Idolatry. Remember, the curses state that the Israelites would remain a pillaged people

---

[94] The Thirteenth Tribe: Arthur Koestler. Pg 60

[95] The Thirteenth Tribe: Arthur Koestler

until the King Messiah returns, and even then, he will only lead the Israelites who turn back to the Torah, and start following it. Again, the litmus test is Torah. Sprinkled amongst the Japhetic, Ashkenazi, Gentile nations, are white complexioned, black bloodline Israelites. Also, there are white converted Israelites. In addition, there are white people who simply just claim to be Israelites.

The issue today that seems to provoke jealousy, or anger, between the white complexioned Israelites, the white people period, and the black complexioned Israelites, is that the whole identity of the bloodline Israelites have been whitewashed in every way except in the Torah, Mishna, and Tanakh. The Torah is very clear regarding Ashkenaz, and it identifies him, and all his progeny as Japhetic Gentiles.

---

96 KJV Bible Genesis 10:5

Yes there is a very real jealousy that occurs when the Torah identifies a nation as Japhetic, and that very Japhetic nation, identifies themselves as Semitic. Then, some members of that Japhetic nation will leave no stone unturned, in order to discredit the very existence of anyone who speaks against the miraculous transfusion of their nationality.

To be clear, this is the prophecy of jealousy, and anger, manifesting itself amongst the Israelites. As previously mentioned, G-D said, "*THEY HAVE MOVED ME TO JEALOUSY WITH THAT THAT IS NOT GOD; THEY HAVE PROVOKED ME TO ANGER WITH THEIR VANITIES: AND I WILL MOVE THEM TO JEALOUSY WITH THOSE WHICH ARE NOT A PEOPLE; I WILL PROVOKE THEM TO ANGER WITH A FOOLISH NATION*"[97] The jealousy manifests itself when one sees a white complexioned, black bloodline Israelite, who is actually trying to keep Torah, attempting to bridge relationships with their black complexioned brethren. Only then, to have a white convert interfere, and attempt to exclude them from a covenant that is not theirs by blood. More specifically, the white converts amongst the Ashkenazi community, attempting to exclude the black bloodline Israelites from the Israelite nation altogether. The anger is further kindled when white supremacists assist in attempting to exclude the black complexioned, bloodline Israelites from their rightful covenant. As prophecy states, the white supremacists do everything in their power to suppress the truth about the Israelites identity.

Lastly, here are pages from the students of Vilma Gaon who was a Jewish sage in the 1700's. These students wrote letters to the bloodline Israelites in Africa, in the years circa 1830 AD. This letter is evidence as to where the Askenazi, Jewish people, understood the Israelites to reside. In this letter they are referred to as the 10 lost tribes, with a full Sanhedren, and a sitting King. As previously written, there absolutely were some, white passing, black bloodline Israelites within the Ashkenazi nation. These passages

---

[97] KJV Bible Deuteronomy 32:21

71

will confirm how the bloodline Israelites, within the Ashkenazi community, viewed their black complexioned, bloodline brethren in Africa.

מלכותם, והמלך יתרומם ויתנשא חרבו יחגור על ירך
גבור הודו והדרו, יצלח וירכב על דבר אמת וענוה
צדק, ותורהו נוראות ימינו, חציו שנונים, עמים תחתיו
יפלו בלב אויבי המלך, כסאך אלדים עולם ועד! שבט
מישר שבט מלכותך, תחת אבתיך יהיו בניך, תשיתמו
לשרים בכל הארץ, תבלנה בשמחות וגיל תבאנה
בהיכל מלך, ואל כבוד אחינו בני ישראל השרים
הצדיקים בית הרכבים בני יהונדב בן רכב אשר נבא
ירמיהו הנביא עליהם "לכן כה אמר ה' צבאות אלדי
ישראל לא יכרת איש ליונדב בן רכב עמד לפני כל
הימים".

Thus send the dwellers of the land of Israel, who abide by the Torah of Moses, [which is] a gift and inherited portion, to our brothers - the children of Israel, the son of Isaaq the son of Abraham who revealed the belief in Hashem - they are our holy and pure brothers, the righteous upon whom the world rests - the Bnei Moshe, servant of Hashem - who dwell across the river Shevatyon also known as Sambatyon, and who pledge allegiance to the king – the King of Israel – who sits upon a mighty throne and who rules over the Ten Tribes, whose settlement is in the land of beyond the rivers of Nubia (Kush), who camp according to their banners, the tribe of Dan, of Naftali, of Gad and Asher, the tribe of Issachar who understand the movements of the celestial bodies – constantly involved in Torah study - and the tribe of Zebulun encamped at Mt. Friyan(?), and across them: the tribe of Reuven, of Efrayim and Menashe, and the tribe of Shimon, may Hashem be with them...and their King...and to our honored brothers, the children of Israel: the upright and righteous sons of Jehonadav the son of Rekhav, upon whom the prophet Jeremiah prophesied, "Therefore said Hashem Z-vaot G-d of Israel, no male offspring of Jonadav ben Rekhav will ever be cut off from standing before me for eternity."

72

ולתהלה בכל עמי הארץ בשובי את שבותיכם לעיניכם
אמר ה'".

Accept abundant greetings from your brethren, the
children of Israel, the last remnant of the tribes of Judah,
Benjamin and Levi, dispersed among the four corners of
the earth; and from your brethren in the Land of Israel
from the diaspora of the land of Ashkenaz, who out of
their burning desire for the holy land - the land adored
by the higher and lower: land of Israel holiest of lands,
put their lives on the line and have left their home
countries and families, and have traversed seas and
deserts until reaching our holy city Jerusalem, and the
burial place of our fathers, that is Hebron, and to the
holy city [of changed name] Tzfat, attaching themselves
to the plot of Hashem and rolling in its dust, who sit in
the tents of the houses of study of Torah and divine
worship, they all send regards as abundant as the dew
and the mist, to endeared brothers and friends,
champions of Torah and mitzvot. Our hearts yearn, our
hearts thirst, our hearts desire to see their faces, to kiss
the dust of their feet, and to witness the grand
countenance of our master the king pure and holy, and
to hear of their wellbeing and their encampment, and
may their eyes witness as ours when Hashem returns to
Zion, and the prophesy of Isaiah the prophet become
fulfilled "saying: to the imprisoned – go free; those in
darkness – to the light."....[more psukim]...

כה אמרו אחיכם ישראל, "מה טובו אהליך יעקב   5
משכנתיך ישראל", אשר מראש מקדמי ארץ שמועה
שמענו כי בחר ה' בהם ויחסם בצל כנפיו ולא הסיר
שבט המושל מאתם, והוד מלכות ישראל נגה עליהם,
ולצדק ימלוך מלך עליהם, ואין עליהם קול נוגש
מאומות העולם, כאשר אבותינו ספרו לנו ורבותינו
הקדושים העידו, אשר בא לפניהם בזמן שש מאות
וארבעים לאלף החמשי איש אחד צדיק וישר, שמו
רבי אלדד הדני משבט דן, והוא ספר והודיע יקר

73

ברורה בידם מפי משה רבנו ע"ה מסיני כפי קבלתם,
ודנים דיני קנסות ודיני נפשות בסנהדרין בפקודתם,
וברוכים באורך ימים ועושר וכבוד מפרי עסק תורתם,
כאשר אמר המלך שלמה ע"ה "ארך ימים בימינה
בשמאלה עשר וכבוד" כברכתם.

Thus said your brothers: "how pleasant are your tents, O
Jacob" - as we have heard from afar that Hashem has
chosen them and protected them and has allowed them
to retain the ruler's staff and they remain [politically]
independent, and have a king who rules them, and don't
suffer from the nations of the world. As our Rabbis have
told us, that in the year 4640 (780 c.e.) a man, one
righteous and upright, from the tribe of Dan, Eldad
Hadani, testified of their greatness and grandeur,
righteousness and holiness saying that Hashem has
helped them remain secure in their settlement, safe from
the surrounding nations, and that the ways of our holy
Torah clear to them as transmitted by Moses our teacher
at Sinai, and that they adjudicate capital and civil cases
in their council, and have reaped the rewards of
longevity prosperity and honor, as Solomon said...

לזכר זאת תעלוזנה כליותינו ותשמח נפשנו, על אשר   6
זכינו לידע כי נתקיים הכתוב "לא אלמן ישראל ויהודה
מאלהיו", כי "עד רד עם אל ועם קדושים נאמן",
ותחזק נפשנו לקול זרים האומרים לנו אין תוחלת
ותקוה, ואומרים איה אליהיכם ויושיעכם, אבדה שם
הגוי הקדוש, נעשינו ללעג ולקלס בגוים, כצאן לטבה
יובל, להרג ולאבד ולמכה ולחרפה, וכל עיר על תלה
בנויה ועיר האלהים מושפלת עד שאול תחתיה, וכל
גוי ועם ממלכתם קיימת ומלכם בראשם ועם ה' אלה
נתונים למשיסה וישראל לבוזזים, הלא ה' זו חטאנו
לו, ואמרנו נגזרנו אבדנו חלילה. אבל בהתאמת לנו
עוז מקל תפארת מלכותם ותוקפם וגבורתם וארצם
הרחבה והמלאה כל טוב ועשרם ומלחמתם וממשלתם

יובל, לההרג ולאבד ולמכה ולחרפה, וכל עיר על תלה
בנויה ועיר האלהים מושפלת עד שאול תחתיה, וכל
גוי ועם ממלכתם קיימת ומלכם בראשם ועם ה' אלה
נתונים למשיסה וישראל לבוזזים, הלא ה' זו חטאנו
לו, ואמרנו נגזרנו אבדנו חלילה. אבל בהתאמת לנו
עז מקל תפארת מלכותם ותוקפם וגבורתם וארצם
הרחבה והמלאה כל טוב ועשרם ומלחמתם וממשלתם
ופחדם על הגוים מסביבם, מה נאוו על ההרים קול
מבשר משמיע שלומם מבשר טוב משמיע ישועתם,
קול צופיך נשאו קול יחדיו ירננו כי עין בעין יראו
בשוב ה' ציון ובחר עוד בירושלם, ועלו מושיעים בהר
ציון.

At the mention of this my innards rejoice and my heart
is gladdened, as we have merited to witness the fruition
of the scripture, "Israel nor Judah are widowed from
their God", and our spirits are strengthened vis a vis
foreigners who say, as we have been led as sheep to
slaughter to be decimated: there is no hope nor salvation
and "where is your God let him come and save you", and
we are disgraced; and all cities are built and standing, yet
the city of God is downtrodden and in ruins, and each
nation has political independence with a king to rule it,
and this nation of Hashem is left to to be trodden upon
and pillaged, to the point where we have declared that
we can be no longer...Yet the staff of their majesty and
might and their vast bountiful lands and their wealth
and success in war, how pleasant is the voice of the
messenger over the hills who brings us these tidings, as
we will have witnessed with our very own eyes Hashem's
salvation of Zion and he shall choose Jerusalem once
more as redeemers shall ascend mount Zion.

אמנם כן מפני כי נתרחקנו מהם במקומותם לשמותם
בארצותם למושבותם, וגדר דרכינו בגזית נתיבותינו
עוה, אסירים קראו למו וישראל שה פזורה נדחה
קראו לה, וידל ישראל מאד וימשלו בהם אויביהם

שורחים שליח ישר והגון, החכם השלם רב' ברוך בן
שמואל מעיד קדש קדש גליל העליון, מסר נפשו לנוד
בארצות בימים ומדברות עד יעזרהו הרחמן לבא לפני
כסא גדולתם.

As we have relied on the words of our sages, "do not
discredit anything", and as our holy teacher R' Shimon
bar Yohai revealed to us in his Zohar, in the days
preceding the coming of Moshiach some of our brethren
of the ten tribes will be discovered, and likewise our
Rabbis have a tradition regarding the scripture stated by
King David, "Gilead is mine, Menashe is mine, the Holy
One blessed be he said to the men of Yabesh Gilead [on
the eastern bank of the Jordan], 'you have performed a
kindness with Saul and his sons, so too will I reward
your offspring in the future', therefore when the holy one
blessed be he gathers Israel, he does so first with the
tribe of Menashe, as it says Gilead is mine, Menashe is
mine" (Yalkut Tehilim 779); and as each endeavor
initially requires an effort from below, and also as our
Rabbis have commented on the scripture "my uncle you
are beautiful – at the time you exact revenge from the
nations, pleasant too - when you reward those who fear
you, our bed - these are the ten tribes who have been
exiled to beyond the Sambatyon, whom the diaspora of
Judah and Benjamin will in the future go and bring, so
that they will merit together the experience of Moshiach
and life in the world to come, as it says, in those days
the house of Judah will go to the house of Israel and
they shall arrive together from the land of the north to
the land I have given to your forefathers." (yalkut song
of songs 985). Therefore we have found the strength, we
the Ashkenazi community in the land of Israel, and are
dispatching to you an upright and wise emissary Rabbi
Baruch ben Shmuel from the holy city of Tzfat, who is
willing to endanger himself and cross seas and deserts
until the Merciful One shall bring him before your great
throne.

והנה עתה תחלה נודיעם בקצרה ממצב כלל אחב"י [10]

In light of all of the above, we request three things from his majesty Our Master the King of Israel , and from our most holy brethren the Bnei Moshe and from all our brothers, the Ten Tribes.

אחת, נפשנו בשאלתנו ועמנו בבקשתנו, על כל כנסת 15 ישראל אשר דל כבודנו בנוים ושקצונו כטומאת הנדה, ושמו הקדוש ית"ש מתחלל באמרם אי אלהיכם ועזרכם, אפס כחנו, נתבלבלה דעתנו ומחשבתנו, וקצר רוחנו לשפוך נפשנו בתפלה ובתחנונים לפני המקום ב"ה, כי נתקיים בנו "ושכרת ולא מיין", כאשר אמר התנא ראב"ע יכול אני לפטור את כל העולם כולו מן הדין תפלה מיום שחרב בהמ"ק ועד עכשיו, שנאמר "לכן שמעי נא זאת עניה ושכרת ולא מיין", ואף כי עתה בדור האחרון הזה, אשר הצרות תכופות וחדלו הפרנסות, ועם ה' אלה נתונים בסתר המדרגה, כי על כן הננו מתנפלים ומתחננים לפני אדונינו: חננו חננו נא אתם אחינו, בני אב אחד נחנו, עזרונו עזרונו בתפלה, כאשר עזר אבישי בן צרוי' לדוד המלך ע"ה בעת צרתו, כמ"ש "ויעזר לו אבישי בן צרוי'", ואמר ר"י אמר רב בקבלתו שעזרו בתפלה, ואם שם היה מאיש אחד לאחד, אף כי מרבים לרבים ועל כבוד קדושת שמו ותורתו ועדתו, כי כשל כח הסבל החירופים והגדופים לשם ה' צבאות, ועד מתי יהי' עוזו בשבי ותפארתו ביד צר ולא יעמוד ברחוק מאתנו ולא יעלים לעתות בצרה? ואם קצף הוא מעט בעד חטאת עמו, הם הוסיפו יותר מהעיקר כפלי כפלים, עולם הקשה וקושי השעבוד, ועברו על השבועה אשר השביעם ה' אלהינו שלא ירבו קושי שעבודם על ישראל, שלא ימהרו הקץ (מדרש רבות שה"ש), וכך אמרו אבותינו ורבותינו בתפלתם: רצוננו לעשות רצונך, ומי מעכב, שאור שבעיסה ושעבוד מלכיות, אשר ע"י שעבוד הקשה ושאין מניחים להגדיל

77

First, we plead with you on behalf of the entire congregation of Israel, whose dignity has been trampled upon, and his holy name which has become desecrated, as we are asked 'where is your God?', our energies are depleted and our minds clouded and have not the strength to pray effectively before our creator as the scripture says 'you have become drunk – but not from wine, and as the tanna R' Eleazar ben Azaria said,"From the day the temple has been destroyed onwards, I can exempt the entire world from prayer, as it says '..you have become drunk - but not from wine'", and now, in the later generations, as the tribulations are more frequent and sustenance is hard to come across...we thereby beseech our master, help us! Oh help us! You are our brothers, we are the sons of one man, aid us, aid us in prayer! As Avishai ben Zruyah helped King David when he was in straits as it says 'And Avishai ben Zruyah aided him' on which the gemara says "R' Yehuda said in the name of Rav, that his help was that he prayed for him", and if that was just for one man by another man, how much more so would it be if it was one congregation for another congregation......and The Creator will help as the suffering we've endured from the nations has been more than requisite and they have transgressed the oath that Hashem bound them by that they shouldn't add to the difficulty of the exile. Thus have our fathers prayed "our desire is to do your desire but the yeast in the dough and subjugation to the nations prevent this from happening": Through the subjugation to the nations it's easier for satan to get the chosen people to sin, and so our rabbis have brought three verses from the prophets to support this assertion, one from Micah[...]one from Jeremiah[...]and Ezekiel[...]please pray profusely for us ...For if He won't redeem us for our sake he'll do it for His sake, as Rashbi taught us in his Tikkunim that the final redemption will be come for His sake just as the men of the great assembly taught us in their formulation of the daily prayers, 'and brings a redeemer to their descendants for the sake of His name with love'....and our master Rashbi

Second, what our hearts desire, this thing: it is well known from our rabbis (rambam first chapter sanhedrin) that before the messiah comes there must be in the land of Israel a court comprised of those ordained in classical semikha [ordination], yet through our sins and through the harsh decrees of the multiple exiles the ordination has disappeared, and the law is that only an ordained can ordain, and Hashem promised that there will be a high court [bet din] as it says, 'I will restore your judges as it was in the past...afterwards you'll be known as the city of justice, a center of truth; Zion shall be redeemed through justice and its returnees through charity'. And this will happen without a doubt once The Creator helps people become attracted to the Torah before the coming of moshiach, and as we have heard that you have a Sanhedrin - ordained from ordained, as you adjudicate capital cases (seemingly this is not the view of r yehoshua b levi in sanhedrin 14a...) please select some of your ordained wise men to come to Israel to ordain scholars so that we'll have in Israel a court comprised of ordained, because the beginning of the redemption hinges on this, and how appropriate would it be for great personages as they are to come to Israel, the land that the tannas and amoras would kiss....and our rabbis said that whoever dwells in the land his sins are expiated...and, even if he's just walked 4 cubits in it he merits the world to come...[continues with praises for the land from the gemara], and our great rabbis said that living in the land of Israel is considered a positive Torah commandment even today, as we learned in the sifri regarding the verse 'you shall inherit them and live in their land', that "living in the land is equal to all the commandments of the torah"...[another gemara stating so]...and currently the land has respite from the oppression of the nations excepting the tributes that we have to pay the ruler of the land; and even if the Torah didn't permit the nation in its entirety to come to the land [during the exile], nowadays for individuals there is no prohibition, as indeed throughout the generations Jews have come. Furthermore, we have a tradition from

The black complexioned, bloodline Israelites need to remember this is all part of G-D's divine plan. When they find themselves feeling the feelings of discomfort, anger, rage, and jealousy, the ONLY solution is turning to Torah, and surrendering, and comforting oneself in it. The poetic justice of even finding the complexion of the Israelites, is in the black complexioned Israelites being forced to relearn Hebrew in order to find themselves in the Torah, Mishna, and Tanakh. The Torah is the beacon for all Israelites, no matter their complexion. One will be able to identify the Israelites by their adherence to Torah. The litmus test for all of us who have the blood of Abraham flowing in our veins, is our love, and adherence to Torah. Shalom.

REFERENCES

1. Shema
2. Personal Prayer
3. Genesis 6:10
4. Talmud: Pirkei DeRabbi Eliezer 24:1
5. Etymoloogical Dictionary of Biblical Hebrew, Based on the com-
   mentaries of Samson Raphael Hirsch. Matityahu Clark
6. Rabbinical Tradition: Pirkei DeRabbi Eliezer 21:10
7. Rabbinical Tradition: Pirkei DeRabbi Eliezer 22:1
8. Rabbinical Tradition: Pirkei DeRabbi Eliezer 22:1
9. The Book Of Lamech of Cain: Ch:1, verse 4
10. The Book of Enoch: Ch: 106
11. King James Version Bible: Genesis 4:16
12. Rabbinical Commentary on Torah: Chizkuni: Leviticus 13:2
13. Talmudic Tradition: Pirkei DeRabbi Eliezer 24:2
14. King James Version Bible: Genesis 10:1-5
15. Rabbinical Tradition: Pirkei DeRabbi Eliezer 24:1
16. Ibid
17. King James Version Bible: Genesis 10:25
18. Ibid: 10:8-11
19. Rabbinical Tradition: Pirkei DeRabbi Eliezer 24:1
20. King James Version Bible: Genesis: 12:7
21. Ibid: 17:1-3
22. Ibid: 16:3
23. Ibid: 17:20
24. Ibid: 24:15
25. Ibid: 21:21
26. Ibid: 25:1-2
27. Ibid 27:1-46
28. Ibid: 28:9
29. Ibid: 36:2
30. Ibid: 29:1-35
31. Ibid: 31:24
32. Gen. Rabbati, Vayeze, p. 119
33. Inner Space by Rabbi Aryeh Kaplan pg. 66
34. King James Version Bible: Genesis: 41:33
35. Targum Jonathan: Genesis 42:8
36. Steve Rudd Bible Chronology Chart
37. King James Version Bible: Genesis 50:11

38. The Prophecy Society of Atlanta, Timeline- Abraham to Solomon
39. King James Version Bible: Exodus: 2:18-19
40. Steve Rudd Exodus Timeline Chart
41. King James Version Bible: Exodus 12:38
42. Ibid: 34:14-16
43. Ibid: Leviticus: 13:1-3
44. Ibid: 19:27
45. Ibid: Numbers: 5:1-2
46. Ibid: 12:1-12
47. Ibid: Deuteronomy 28:68
48. Ibid:
49. Ibid: 32:26
50. Ibid:
51. Ibid: 30: 19-20
52. Ibid: 31: 16-18
53. Ibid: 32: 20-21
54. British Colonial Law 1664
55. King James Version Bible: 1Samuel 16:12
56. Ibid: 17:42
57. Ibid: Song of Solomon 1:5
58. Ibid: 1:6
59. Ibid:
60. Ibid: 5: 10-11
61. Simple image search
62. King James Version Bible: 2Kings 17:6-23
63. Ibid: Zephaniah 3:10
64. Ibid: 2Kings 24:1-7
65. Ibid: Lamentations 4:8
66. Ibid: 5:10
67. A Timeline of Biblical History
68. "Dio's Rome, Volume V., Book 68, paragraph 32"
69. Ancient Jewish History: The Bar-Kokhba Revolt, Jewish Virtual Library
70. History of the Jews: by Professor H. Graetz VOL. II pg 608
71. Ibid: pg 630
72. Ancient History Encyclopedia: Kahina
73. The Ritual of Eldad Ha-Dani: Reconstructed and Edited From Manuscripts and a Genizah
74. Jewish History: Chabad.org Eldad Ha-Dani
75. The Thirteenth Tribe: Arthur Koestler
76. Ibid: pg. 60
77. The Jews of Khazaria: Keven Alan Brook. pg. 21

78. The Critical Review, Or, annals Of Literature, Volume 57 pg 141
79. Ibid: pg. 142
80. Virginiaplaces.org: The Origins of Slavery in Virginia
81. Image search web: Israel Hill Virginia
82. Codice Casanatense info page.
83. Biblioteca Casanatense: private library
84. Art Treasures of Russia: Harry N. Abrams, INC. Publishers New York
85. Ibid:
86. Ibid:
87. Ibid:
88. Ibid:
89. Ibid:
90. King James Version Bible: Deuteronomy 32:26
91. Ibid: 30:1-9
92. Talmud: Pirkei DeRabbi Eliezer 24:1
93. The Thirteenth Tribe: Arthur Koestler. pg 60
94. Ibid:
95. King James Version Bible: Genesis 10:5
96. Ibid: Deuteronomy 32:21

Made in the USA
Columbia, SC
22 December 2021

52603512R00049